NOBBINS

by Ray Lambert

ISBN 978-0-9544519-4-3

Published by: RAYL, 13 Weedswood Road, Chatham, Kent ME5 0QR
Typeset by Richard Lloyd, Reading

FOREWORD

I have known Ray Lambert ever since I started to receive the Kent Ex-Boxers' Association Newsletter a decade or more ago.

As a proud member of the Sussex Ex-Boxers' Association, which for a time amalgamated with Kent, I receive newsletters from a multitude of EBAs around the country. I always looked forward in particular to the Kent one because of the Ray Lambert column which provided a shot of humour, unique among them all. As a result I started to correspond with Ray and was very pleased to finally get an opportunity to meet him when the Kent Association paid a visit to the Sussex one. I sat and chatted with a very distinguished looking gentleman and told him how I much I enjoyed reading his column. He seemed very appreciative until about 10 minutes into the conversation when he told me he was in fact not Ray Lambert at all! So it was not until much later that we finally got together.

Since then we have continued to correspond and chat on the telephone and he has even managed to persuade me to part with a few of my hard earned pounds to buy a copy of his book 'Nozzers'. Probably out of the sense of guilt, or in a moment of weakness, he recently and very kindly sent me a copy of his follow up book 'Nozzers Go West'.

Since he told me of his plans for this particular book I have really looked forward to it coming out. He is a great one for a joke and has a very wry sense of humour. It is good from time to time that we see that side of our very exciting but bloody sport.

Almost certainly I will have to find the few pounds necessary to purchase the book but I am sure that, in the reading, I, as well as you, will consider it money well spent.

Simon Block
General Secretary
British Boxing Board of Control 2000-2008

By the same author:

Kent Ex-Boxers Association, 'Comes of Age', 1987

Nozzers, 2003

Nozzers First Class, 2004

Nozzers Go West, 2005

PREFACE

As the long standing press officer of the 'Kent Ex-Boxers Association' (Kent EBA) and nowadays life member, it has been my pleasure to have travelled around the country at the invitation of other EBAs and meet like-minded people, former professionals, amateurs and those with a lifelong interest on this sport of ours. It has been a real pleasure to swap yarns – and the occasional pint – with former combatants in our mutual sport; the sport we like to think of as 'The King of Sports'.

I have been absolutely delighted to listen to stories from years gone by, whether they were from champions or from humble undercard boxers, and suddenly it dawned on me that these stories should be collected and written down before they are lost forever. So carried away I have been whilst listening to the stories from the very people that have given us mere spectators first class entertainment over the years, that I had forgotten to write these memories down. Luckily I saw the light and furnished myself with a notebook. These then are my jottings, taken down over the years.

In the main the stories on the following pages are used with the permission of those people named in the stories – the very people who shared their memories with me. To thank those people individually would take another book. I hope this will suffice as a thank you to all concerned.

I have not attempted to cover all the champions and well-known personalities within our sport and some readers may be disappointed that their particular friend or hero does not get a mention. To mention everyone would be impossible and there would still be people missed. This is not a boxing records book but intended more as a light read of some slightly quirky and offbeat stories.

Naturally those of the 1800s and beyond also the first half of the twentieth century for that matter – before my time – were for obvious reasons not recited to me personally. For those stories and anecdotes of the very old timers I am indebted to the king of boxing historians and former editor of Boxing News, Gilbert Odd. Gilbert was kind enough to furnish me with most, if not all, of the old time material before he died, and several of those stories in this book he wrote for me himself.

I started this book several years ago and I hope I will not be judged too harshly if one or two slip-ups have managed to evade my scrutiny. Such things as where a record may have been surpassed as, indeed all records are sooner or later, or where a champion has nowadays gained the prefix former. I have done my best although I admit to a large dose of fallibility.

Memories are precious things but fade with time and sometimes, although well meaning, can tend to distort the facts, nevertheless once they are gone they're gone forever. I hope that I've salvaged a few.

After all, this book is constructed entirely from recycled memories.

Ray Lambert, 2008

A thorn between two roses....

The author flanked by two first class bookends at a former Royal Navy boxers meeting at Croydon on August 26, 1984.

'Seaman' Bill Storrie (left) would certainly have been champion if he had persued his boxing career instead of his naval career, and 'Seaman' Jim Lawlor (right) would definitely have become champion if his opponents were not afraid to meet him in the ring.

All boxers agree that good footwork is an essential part of sparring but how many of them know that the word 'spar' is from the French 'esparer' – to kick.

Seaman Jim Lawlor

' How will they manage without me? '

Sometimes when you are feeling important,
Sometimes when your ego's in bloom,
Sometimes when you take it for granted,
You're the cleverest man in the room.

Sometimes when you feel that your going,
Will leave an unfillable hole,
Just follow this simple instruction,
And see how it humbles your soul.

Take a bucket and fill it with water,
Put your hand in, right up to the wrist,
Take it out and the hole that's remaining,
Is the measure of how much you'll be missed!

Many people have claimed this poem as their own work but it was actually written by 'Seaman' Jim Lawlor, well known boxer of the 1930s and 1940s. Jim, the inventor of the famous 'Lowestoft Loop' a punch that laid many a good man low, was a prolific letter writer and also a keen poet.

On another page is the poem 'WHO' that he penned for Muhammad Ali and was displayed in the gym where Ali used to train under the watchful eye of the famous Angelo Dundee.

'Seaman' Jim Lawlor joined the Royal Navy as a 15 year old in 1927, then sailed and fought his way around the world until he was bought out of the service in 1936, in order to concentrate on his boxing. Although Jim was known as a knock-out specialist, it was not until after he was recalled to uniform for World War II that he scored his most spectacular KO.

He was serving aboard HMS Vesper when, in 1940, they sank the first U-Boat of the war, in the English Channel.

> A riddle posed by Seaman Jim Lawlor asks:
> *Why were a lot of my opponents lazy?*
> *Answer – they didn't get up until after ten!*

'Seaman' Jim Lawlor's first top of the bill bout, scheduled to take place on November 16, 1933, against American Al Miller, at Great Yarmouth, was almost a non event.

Serving aboard a Royal Navy gunboat, 'Seaman' Jim was enjoying an off duty sleep only to wake up and find his ship had put to sea – and his all important top of the bill bout was scheduled for three hours time.

Luckily they were in the vicinity of Great Yarmouth and, when the captain learned of the situation, he put the ship into harbour just along the coast and 'Seaman' Jim was able to keep his appointment.

Lady luck stayed with him that night and Jim KO'd Miller in the fourth round using his famous 'Lowestoft Loop' punch, thereby finishing his first year in the professional ranks undefeated.

~ ~

It was a Jewish Charity Night at the old Blackfriars Ring and the Saturday night house was packed, with the Lord Mayor and several special guests at ringside. In between bouts they were auctioning almost everything they could lay their hands on; paintings, books and even greyhounds were going under the hammer. Excitement was running high and everything else was running late.

'Seaman' Jim Lawlor was waiting at 8.30 pm to fight Rex Whitney, a promising 21 year old from Leicester. At midnight he was still waiting, when into the dressing room came Victor Berliner, the promoter.

'We're running very late,' said Mr B.

'We certainly are,' said Mr L.

'I'll double your purse if you can get it over by a KO in the first,' said Mr B.

'Nuff said,' said Mr L.

Jim said: 'I did what I was told and I won by a KO in the first. I then went to the office to tell the promoter that I had done as he asked. Mr Berliner was very pleased and true to his word he doubled my purse.

Unfortunately things hadn't worked out quite so rosy for young Mr Whitney. Rex was in tears because no-one had knocked him out before.

There have been many stories over the years about friendships between showbiz personalities and the stars of the boxing ring but none as strange as the first time meeting between Jim Lawlor and the comedy duo Flanagan and Allen.

It was the first time at the Blackfriars Ring for 'Seaman' Jim and he was matched against southpaw Welshman Mog Williams. Jim won by a KO in the forth round.

Later, a man came into the dressing room carrying a handful of one pound and ten shilling notes and asking for Seaman Lawlor. He thrust the money at me saying: 'Well done Jim, this is from Bud.'

Jim said: 'I didn't know what to say. I just blurted out: 'Who's Bud?'

The answer was, of course, Bud Flanagan. Bud just loved a gamble and he had seen that I was confident of winning, so he backed me to win. That money was a small fortune to me. It was £25 and my purse for top of the bill wasn't that much!

After that nice gesture I received a lovely Christmas present from them both every Christmas. It was their own calendar with the words: 'Still your humble servants, Flanagan and Allen OY'

'Seaman' Jim Lawlor was one of Britain best welterweights during the 1930s and although he never actually won the championship, he is probably better remembered than many that did. Nowadays, many years later, Jim is still fondly remembered as the man who should have been champion.

The southpaw seaman was a KO specialist and of his total bouts, which came close to the magic century, around half never went the distance. Most of his stoppages were courtesy of his famous 'Lowestoft Loop' – a sharp uppercut to his opponent's midriff.

The ferocity of Lawlor's punching was legendary during his boxing career and after his retirement from the ring he turned to the much gentler pursuit of punching out poetry.

Jim is well remembered for his verse, and 'WHO', the poem he penned for Muhammad Ali, is probably his best known. The tribute that Jim composed when Ali was at his boxing peak is reproduced opposite. He sent it to the champ at his Florida base, where it was given pride of place in Angelo Dundee's Gym. Ali sent Jim a note of thanks and appreciation.

'Seaman' Jim recalled the time when his famous punch the 'Lowestoft Loop' helped him to deal with a crooked manager.

He said: ' I fell out with my manager way back in the 1930s when I discovered that my purses were £20 more than he was telling me. When I got proof that he was robbing me every fight I gave him the Lowestoft Loop and he spent a week in hospital recovering. I sacked him and he moved up to Norwich and became manager of Ginger Sadd. Ginger was fearsome boxer and a couple of years younger than me. That ex-manager died many years ago.'

Jim joined the Royal Navy at HMS Ganges in 1927, as a fifteen year old and it was then that he started his professional career. He won the lightweight title in what was, in those days, a compulsory boxing tournament for all new entries. His instructor was so happy with his achievement that he gave Jim a penny – his first paid bout!

Jim's biggest regret in his formidable career was that he never got a shot at the British title. 'In 1939 my new manager, Alf Jacobs, demanded my right to a shot with the Control Board and in Boxing News, and I wrote pushing my claim to all the major newspapers in the country. Twice I was scheduled to fight Ernie Roderick, the title-holder, but both times when I arrived at the venue he was 'indisposed' and the bout never took place. Like most other welterweights at the time, he was afraid to meet me'.

Jim Lawlor, the southpaw seaman, was certainly stamping his authority on the welterweight division and trying hard to enhance his claim to a British title shot by doing everything in his power to make the boxing authorities take notice of him. Even writing letters to the Control Board and all the leading newspapers, laying out his credentials and demanding his chance, all to no avail.

WHO

by 'Seaman' Jim Lawlor

Who - Is a pugilist, a poet, a preacher.

Who - In all three is the teacher.

Who - Can make you mad and sigh.

Who - Can make you laugh or cry.

Who - Has great personality and charm.

Who - Outside the ring would do you no harm.

Who - Is known everywhere.

Who - Makes all people stand and stare.

Who - Invented the words 'Super Fame'.

Who - Has magic in his name.

Who - Has earned in the sporting race.

Who - Has still retained his handsome face.

Who - Walks with Kings, Princes and Presidents too.

Who - Can tell governments what to do.

Who - Treats everyone the same.

Who - Is a credit to the boxing game.

Who - Has everyone watching him – 'his fan'.

Who - Is a truly remarkable man.

Who - Lifted the fight game off the floor.

Who - Loves all people rich and poor.

Who - Put all the heavyweights in the big money.

Who - Beat them all to make it funny.

Who - Gave the great trainer Angelo Dundee most fame.

Who - Gave drew Bundini Brown more of the same.

Who - Has been a legend for many years now.

Who - Soon will retire (from the ring) and take a final bow.

Who - Always will be 'The Greatest', it's so plain to see.

Who - The former Cassius Marcellus Clay, known today as

'The Super Supreme'

MUHAMMAD ALI

In November 1936 'Seaman' Jim took on and beat Chris Dawson, in Norwich and then travelled 500 miles to Plymouth to take Charlie Parkin the full ten rounds distance just 24 hours later.

He still didn't impress the Control Board but Boxing Magazine recognised the feat and awarded him a Certificate of Merit for the best performance of the week.

CERTIFICATE OF MERIT

"THE WATCHER'S" award for the best performance of the week goes to JIM LAWLOR of Lowestoft for knocking out Chris Dawson in one round at Norwich on 12th November, 1936, and within 24 hours outpointing Battling Parkin at Plymouth. 500 miles travelling —two victories.

Ex-Seaman
JIM LAWLOR
of
Lowestoft
a great puncher of the 1930s

After the fifth time of winning the world title, Ray Robinson was asked what he did different this time that he didn't do in his last bout. He replied: 'I won the world championship!'

Former world heavyweight champ George Foreman asked the pertinent question: 'What's the point in weighing heavyweights?'

Swedish newspapers pilloried Ingemar Johansson after his disqualification in the 1952 Olympic Games boxing final – saying that his boxing career was over. Seven years later it was a different story when he became professional heavyweight world champion taking the title from Floyd Patterson in three rounds, in New York.

John Ashton, middleweight battler of the early 1990s, had good training for his roadwork; he spent his formative years pounding the roads as a policeman.

Unfortunately his roadwork advantage didn't give him an advantage over his opponents and, after four unsuccessful attempts to arrest a title, John announced his retirement from the ring in February 1993.

Something like fifty years after Welshman Tommy Farr took Joe Louis a full fifteen rounds before losing a close decision in New York, Tommy cracked: 'Whenever Joe Louis is mentioned, my nose starts to bleed.'

Oscar Gardner put Terry McGovern on the deck with a belt to the jaw in the first round of their March 1900 bout. In an effort to beat the count McGovern grabbed Gardners legs to pull himself upright and by the time the referee had finished telling him that was not allowed 14 seconds had elapsed.

McGovern took advantage of the referee's generosity to turn the tables on Gardner, knocking him out in the third round to win the bout.

After a very short cruiserweight unification bout between David Hey and Enizo Macinelli, at London's newly named O2 Centre – the ill fated Millennium Dome – new champion Hey stated the obvious when he said: 'It was a contest between two hard punchers.'

Hey stopped Macinelli before the end of the second round to become WBC, WBO and WBA titleholder and then added: 'Pound for pound, I am the hardest puncher in the world!'

When Max Baer won the world heavyweight championship by defeating Primo Carnera, on June 14, 1934 at Long Island, New York, he did so in great style by putting the Italian giant down eleven times in eleven rounds.

British Boxing Board of Control standard weights that apply to professional boxing:

Flyweight	8 stones and under
Super Flyweight	8 stones 3 pounds and under
Bantamweight	8 stones 6 pounds and under
Super Bantamweight	8 stones 10 pounds and under
Featherweight	9 stones and under
Super Featherweight	9 stones 4 pounds and under
Lightweight	9 stones 9 pounds and under
Light Welterweight	10 stones and under
Welterweight	10 stones 7 pounds and under
Light Middleweight	11 stones and under
Middleweight	11 stones 6 pounds and under
Super Middleweight	12 stones and under
Light Heavyweight	12 stones 7 pounds and under
Cruiserweight	14 stones 4 pounds and under
Heavyweight	Any weight

Bob Fitzsimmons fought his final bout against Don Sweeny in 1913. It was a six rounder and Bob was 52. Bob died in Chicago four year later, aged 56.

Roberto Duran has achieved 20 first round knockouts in his 86 bouts.

Bantamweight Jim Higgins holds the record for the fastest National Sporting Club Belt outright win of 11 months and 6 days. His three notches came on February 23 1920, November 29, 1920 and January 31, 1921

The night Joe Louis was challenged for the world heavyweight title by Welshman Tommy Farr, in Yankee Stadium, New York an array of talent was invited into the ring and introduced to the 32,000 crowd.

Among those in that historic line up on August 30, 1937, were seven former world heavyweight champions.

The line up included such well remembered notables as: Arthur Donovan (referee), Jack Johnson, Jim Braddock, Sixto Escobar, Ceferino Garcia, Fred Apostoli, Benny Leonard, Lou Ambers, Barney Ross, Pedro Montanery, Jack Sharkey, Mickey Walker, Gene Tunney, Jack Dempsey, Marcel Thil, Max Baer, Max Schmeling and Johnny Dundee.

When promoter Jack Solomons died, he left the British Boxing Board of Control the sum of one penny in his will.

When Rinty Monaghan beat Dado Marino for the world flyweight title at Harringay, London on October 6, 1947, America and Rinty's native Eire recognised the bout as for the championship but the BBBofC insisted Jackie Patterson was the official world champion.

Monaghan settled all doubts by going after Patterson and beating him as well.

Andy Bowen, the man who, in 1893, took part in the longest recorded fight ever, was killed a year later when he took part in a contest and was knocked down by his opponent and banged his head so hard that he died from concussion.

There are ten boxers who have more than one hundred knockouts to their credit. Starting with Jimmy Wilde with exactly 100. Next comes Henry Armstrong with 101; Sandy Sadler 103; Jack Fox 104; Ray Robinson 110; George Odwell 114; Sam Langford 118; Billy Bird 125; Young Stribling 126 and 'Ageless' Archie Moore who tops the list with 129.

Henry Armstrong won world titles at three different weights and held them all at the same time. They were featherweight (October 29, 1937); lightweight (August 17, 1938) and welterweight (May 31, 1938). All three titles were won within a ten month period.

Henry went on to successfully defend his world welterweight crown an incredible twenty-one times in two and a half years, between May 31, 1938 and October 4, 1940.

Joe Grim is a boxer that not too many people will easily bring to mind, although in his day he was a very busy ring warrior.

In a ten year career up until 1913, Joe fought more than 300 bouts meeting such notables as Jack O'Brien, Bob Fitzsimmons, Tommy Burns, Joe Gans, Sam McVey etc. and was only ever knocked out three times.

Unfortunately Mr Grim had a less auspicious claim to fame – of his 300 plus bouts, he only won five!

When Jack Petersen took the British light heavyweight title from Harry Crossley on May 23, 1932, the Lonsdale Belt couldn't be found. Lord Lonsdale was at ringside on that night and he presented Jack with a cup instead.

In 1986 when Jack Petersen was elected president of the British Boxing Board of Control he was still concerned about that missing Belt.

Meanwhile that elusive Belt had reappeared in New Zealand and was given to the Queen on her tour of that country in the early 1980s.

Upon her return Her Majesty gave the Belt back to the BBBofC.

Jack recalled: 'Crossley beat Frank Moody to get the title and both their names are on it. But years later when that particular Belt turned up again, my name still never got added.'

Coppernob

Tom McCarthy's book 'Boysie', which highlighted 'The worst street in North London', Campbell Bunk, Islington, as it was between the two World Wars, gave a very vivid portrayal of the Smith brothers, John and Joe who lived there at the time.

The extract read thus:

'On other occasions the cry 'they're at it again' would announce the fact that the Smith brothers had squared up to each other again and were about to slug it out in the street. Hearing the commotion I would rush down the stairs into the middle of the road and, sure enough, people would be gathering in the street, usually outside Pococks shop. I would join the rush and wiggle my way to the front of the crowd, which in no time at all had formed a circle round the two big ginger haired brothers.

The two of them would fight it out with bare fists until one was out cold. Everyone crowded to the scene, not caring why the fight had started in the first place, only interested in a bit of free entertainment. You chose the brother you fancied to win and cheered him on, no one cared who the wronged one was, 'Come on coppernob' could be heard from all round the crowd, that was neutral enough as both of them were coppernobs. Both brothers were over six feet tall and well built, I remember one had his hair parted in the middle, they looked every bit as good as two heavyweight boxers.

The excitement in the crowd would be at fever pitch and the arena, that is the space in the middle of the crown in this case, got smaller and smaller as people at the back pushed forward in their efforts to see what was going on. The seconds, friends of the brothers, would push the crowd back using a clothes line pinched from a back yard to keep the area clear, buckets and sponges had been brought out with which to revive the fighters so that they could carry on fighting. All the upper windows overlooking the scene were soon packed with people, they were the equivalent of ringside seats; bets were being laid as fast as the bookies could handle the cash. The police had broken up the fight last time and it had been declared a draw, there were no points scored in this fight, no referee either! The end of each round came when one or other had been knocked to the ground. It must have been like one of the old prizefights before the Marquis of Queensbury got busy!

Joe and Johnny Smith really used to paste the hell out of each other and it didn't take long to get their faces covered in blood. When a particularly

12

good thump one on his arse among the front row a brief interval was signalled and the second got busy with the sponge and cold water, giving instructions how to improve on the pulverizing of his opponent. All the time the crowd would be yelling and cheering: 'Give 'im a fourpenny one, Joe.' 'Go on Johnny my son, sock 'im one.'

As the two brothers slugged away at each other, so their faces and bodies would begin to show signs of the punishment they were taking. Red and bluish-black patches would appear with blood smeared from cuts and bleeding noses all over them, not a sight for weak stomachs! Sometimes fights started in the crowd between rival supporters just to add to the general confusion and then it wasn't safe to be little and in the centre of an excited crowd, so I would wiggle and push my way to a safer part, sometimes crawling on all fours among the blood and snot on the pavement! By the time round twenty or so came and both men had been knocked down but not out, both men would be in bad shape and the pavement awash with water and splattered blood. One good blow would all that was needed now to bring about victory for one brother and a selection of punters; sometimes at this stage the brother would call it a day and shake hands, grinning and holding each other up as they staggered back to their house. Once the fight was over the crowd soon dispersed and all that was left was the wet and blood-splattered pavement. I don't suppose Harringay Arena ever put on a boxing show as good as these fights, and these were free!'

John (L) and Joe (R) Smith at the time of the launch
of the book 'Boysie' that carried the Coppernob story

The fourth of July 1919 proved to be no holiday for Jess Willard when Jack Dempsey soundly beat him for the world heavyweight championship.

Willard lost more than his dignity on that occasion in Toledo, Ohio in what was possibly the worst beating a defending world champion had ever taken. Big Jess, almost 60 pounds heavier than Dempsey, lost a lot of claret, two teeth and his title, the title that he had held for more than four years.

Willard was on the canvas for the seventh time in the first round when he was saved by the bell. Dempsey thought he had won and left the ring but was called back. He then continued the devastation of the six feet six and a quarter inch 245 pounds champion for another two rounds. Then, during the third round interval, Willard announced from his stool that he could not continue.

Jimmy Edgar had the distinction of having his bout with the legendary Jake LaMotta voted 'Fight of the Year' by the New York press, in 1942.

All the more impressive considering his introduction to boxing was 'just to make the numbers up for a sparring session.'

When Jack Dempsey fought Bill Brennan he hit him on the jaw with such force that the blow broke Brennans ankle.

Georges Carpentier, the well remembered and well liked world champion from France, won every French title from flyweight up to light heavyweight.

The longest fight on record took place in New Orleans in 1893, between Andy Bowen and Jack Burke.

It started at 9.15 pm on the evening of April 6 and went on until the 110 round ended at 4.19 am on April 7. By this time both men had received quite a beating and the referee refused to allow them to start another round. Instead he declared the result a draw.

The two men were fighting for a purse of $2,500, which was quite a substantial amount in those days and, as neither of them was keen to repeat the performance, they shared the purse money between them.

Straight after his success in the 1990 ABA championships, flyweight Johnny Armour turned professional.

By coincidence, his first three professional opponents were Mexican.

Kid Lewis and Freddie Welsh both lost their respective world titles in so-called no decision bouts.

14

When the National Sporting Club engaged Sam Langford to box Iron Hague in 1909, the coloured man was asked, with the customary courtesy, if he had any preference as to who should referee the bout.

'No sah,' said Sam. 'I have brought my own referee.'

'But that's not permitted,' the horrified club manager told him. 'You must have a member as referee but you can make your own choice from among them.'

'This is my referee, boss,' answered Langford shaking a large right fist under the managers nose. 'No one argues with him.'

Langford got his own way and went on to knock out the British champion in four rounds.

Ted 'Kid' Lewis and Jack Britton fought each other an incredible twenty seven times in the six years between 1914 and 1920.

Kid Freeman undefeated featherweight champion of Kent in the 1930s remembered the time he was brassed off with the ribbing that he was taking.

He was boxing at The Casino, Rochester, Kent and getting pretty sore around the ribs. 'Kid' complained to the referee but was told in no uncertain terms to carry on and get on with it.

However, half way through the contest it became obvious that something was amiss as red wheals began to appear around the Kid's mid section.

The referee stopped the bout and ordered the opponent to remove his right glove, which revealed an enormous brass ring.

'What's that?' enquired the referee.

'I wear it for sentimental reasons,' was the innocent reply.

Offending ring removed, the bout continued.

Ernie Woodman, the Battersea heavyweight who was a firm favourite with the fans at The Ring Blackfriars between the wars, finally became old enough to legally enter a pub and buy a pint in 1988. For, at long last Ernie had reached the ripe old age of 18.

Ernie was a leap-year baby and insisted upon only counting his birthdays, which, of course, is every fourth year.

His newly gained entitlement didn't affect him very much though because Ernie was almost teetotal.

Before his sudden death in January 1989, Ernie was a bookie and only went into pubs to collect bets and to attend meetings of ex-boxers associations all over the country, in his capacity as chairman of the Sussex Ex-Boxers Association.

Welsh heavyweight Tommy Farr had five bouts whilst in the USA. The one that everyone remembers was his fine performance against Joe Louis, whom he took to the full 15 rounds distance, in New York on August 30, 1937, in a world championship bout.

But while he was on that side of the Atlantic he also met James J Braddock, Max Baer, Lou Nova and Red Burman.

Australia has long featured their share of world class boxing but until Dennis Andries defended his WBC light heavyweight title against English born domiciled Aussie Guy Waters in Adelaide, on January 19, 1991, there had never been a world title fight staged in that town before.

The bout took place in the open air on the tennis courts in Memorial Drive and Andries won on points over the twelve rounds route. He was taking part in his eighth title bout.

Fancy taking part in a bout and then having to wait until the following year to learn the referees decision.

It is not as daft as it appears.

On December 31, 1923, Danny Frush and Billy Matthews engaged in a fast and furious battle at the old Blackfriars Ring. The bout contained numerous fouls, low blows and, at times, both contestants scrambling about on the canvas. In the fifth round the contest was called to a premature halt in the interests of preventing a riot in the crowd and the MC announced that the referee would give his verdict later.

As it transpired Frush insisted upon another doctor being sent for to examine his injuries he had sustained through alleged low blows. This, naturally, took quite a while to arrange.

The following morning (January 1) a notice appeared outside the venue declaring Frush had got the verdict and Matthews was disqualified.

The bout took place in 1923 and the verdict was announced in 1924.

I'm the most famous person that I know. So says Hector Comacho. Maybe he should get out more.

English boxer Charlie Mitchell's claim to fame was that he held the famous John L Sullivan to a draw over 39 rounds when they met in France on March 10, 1888. But before that, in America, Mitchell had the distinction of being the first boxer to knock Sullivan off his feet.

Best Wishes
Jack Petersen

HEAVYWEIGHT
CHAMPION OF GREAT BRITAIN
JULY 12TH. 1932

Ernie Woodman

Film and Television

The Smith brothers, John and Joe, can lay claim to having been boxing ambassadors on British television. They did a mock up bout in a ring at Alexandra Palace, in October 1938. This was in order for those early days television technicians to get their contrasts and shadows correct. The Smith boys were there for a week, working under the direction of television pioneer Sir John Baird – and for their help they were both given a beer tankard and a five-pound note.

The first boxing show ever to be filmed turned out to be a complete waste of time. It was scheduled for February 21, 1896, between Bob Fitzsimmons and Peter Maher, in Langtry, Texas. But Fitzsimmons spoilt the show when he knocked out Maher early in the first round before the cameras were even running.

A year later, March 17, 1897 Fitzsimmons made amends by appearing in the first ever championship fight to be filmed. In Nevada he KOd James J Corbett in the 14th round, to take the world heavyweight championship.

We had to wait then for fifty years until December 5, 1947, for the first ever heavyweight championship to be televised. This was at Madison Square Gardens, New York and Joe Louis beat Jersey Joe Walcott over the 15 rounds points route.

The result was the same twelve years later when the first colour television world championship bout was screened, again at Madison Square Gardens, on December 10, 1965. This time it was the turn of the welters and Emile Griffith beat Manuel Gonzalez over 15 rounds.

~ 🕴 ~

The first championship boxing to be televised was the well-documented Eric Boon v Arthur Danahar, lightweight title bout on February 23, 1939, at Harringay.

But contrary to popular belief this was not the first televised boxing. Danahar was in action 'on the tube' about five months previously when he faced Pancho Martinez, on a NSC bill from Earls Court, on October 3, 1938. Only the first three rounds were broadcast on that occasion.

However, old records inform us that a full five years before that Archie Sexton and Laurie Raiteri boxed three rounds on television although there can't be many people left who can remember the occasion. Plus, of course, television being what it was in those days, there can't have been many people that actually watched it at the time.

When James J Jefferies fought Jack Johnson in Reno, in July 1910, author Jack London covered the fight for the New York Herald.

He did daily articles on both boxers for ten days previous to the fight and then reported on the contest itself.

John Smith was called-up into the army and swiftly became a force to be reckoned with in service boxing circles, soon becoming the Imperial Services welterweight champion.

'I asked if I could take home the cup I had won to show my family,' John said. The army gave him a 48-hour pass and he took the cup home and proudly showed it around his family and neighbours and friends. All went well until it was time to return to his barracks and there was no sign of the cup, it was nowhere to be found.

John recalled:' A lot of nervous nail biting and head scratching followed until the truth came out – my dad had pawned it!'

In 1955 Jack Solomons, the noted British fight promoter, said: 'I will never allow my chief fight to be televised.'

The life and times of Lionel Rose, the Australian bantamweight who went on to world honours in 1968, has been recorded on film in Australia.

Fight fans all over the world will get a second chance to marvel at the exploits of the little Aborigine, when the mini series hits the television screens.

Bob Fitzsimmons was born in 1863; the same year that old time boxer Jem Mace was world champion.

In later years Mace brought Ruby Robert into boxings limelight by inviting him to take part in a tournament that he (Mace) was promoting. Fitz stole the show by dispatching five opponents on that same night and all by Knockout.

In a remarkable boxing career that lasted an incredible 34 years, Fitzsimmons met and beat the best, including the famous Non-Pareil, Jack Dempsey and of course James J Corbett, from whom he took the world title.

A young boxer was trying hard to fight off an attack of nerves as he waited in his corner for his bout to start. It did nothing to allay his trepidation when he noticed the famous Jack Dempsey in his opponents corner.

In an effort to ease the tension, his cornerman told him: 'It's OK lad, you don't have to fight him!'

Peter Kane won the flyweight championship of the world on September 22, 1938 but was unable to take the British crown. He moved up to bantamweight and took the European and Empire titles but was still not able to win the British crown.

In the mid 1930s he put together an incredible string of forty-one winning bouts.

After Bob Fitzsimmons left the middleweight division to compete in the heavyweight bracket, Tommy Ryan relinquished his welterweight title and claimed the middleweight championship but this proved not to have been a very wise move because he was beaten by his very first challenger.

Kid McCoy KO'd him and took the title but McCoy never defended and soon moved up to try his luck among the heavies, leaving Ryan to reclaim the title and, having been given a second chance, this time he made no mistake and successfully repelled six challengers before retiring in 1907.

Peter Rudemacher challenged world heavyweight champion Floyd Patterson for the world title in his first ever professional bout.

Rudemacher, former Olympic Games heavyweight champion of 1956, fought Patterson in Seattle on August 22, 1957, in what was billed as the amateur heavyweight champion versus the professional heavyweight champion.

For his trouble Rudemacher was KO'd in the sixth round, after being on the deck seven times. He managed to floor Patterson for a brief count in the second round but that was his only success. For even at the payout Peter was still the loser.

Records show that Patterson received a quarter of a million dollars for the fight but Rudemacher got nothing for his services and his backers also lost heavily.

J. Paul Getty, said to have been the world's richest man in his day, certainly knew the financial business. But what is not so well known is his keen interest in the weightlifting and boxing business.

Getty came to England in 1927 and soon formed an association with WA 'Bill' Pullum that lasted right up until Bill's death in 1960, at the age of 74.

The big rich man and the small cockney used to meet at the Camberwell Weightlifting Club, in London and Bill, the nine stone weightlifting World Champion who held 192 weightlifting records, taught Getty all he needed to know about tossing the iron.

To cultivate his interest in boxing Getty also went to the best. His boxing tutor was none other than soon-to-be world champion, Jack Dempsey. Three years before Dempsey's devastation of James J Willard in 1919 for the world heavyweight title, he and Getty used to spar in California – and Getty has the distinction of being the only man ever to have KO'd the champ.

Years later Dempsey recalled that record spoiling KO. 'We used to double date and we only ever quarrelled once. That was when we both wanted the same girl. Paul threw a feint with his right and knocked me senseless with a left uppercut – the first and only time I have ever been completely out in my life.'

Two American boxers tie for the honours of the most consecutive knockouts. The record is 43. LeMar Clark and Billy Fox share the record. Fox achieved this remarkable feat in the late 1940s and Clark emulated Fox a decade later.

Ironically both boxers run was brought to an end when they were KO'd themselves, each by a distinguished opponent: Fox by Gus Lesnevich and Clark by Muhammad Ali.

World heavyweight champion, John L Sullivan, who made the successful transition from bare knuckles to gloves, was a very popular boxer whose fame spread around the world.

On his way to France to fight England's Charlie Mitchell in Chantilly, on March 10, 1888, he stopped off in England en route and the Prince of Wales (later to become King Edward VII) asked to meet him.

After being introduced, Sullivan boxed an exhibition with British Champion Jem Smith, in front of the Prince, at the Guards Barracks off Birds Cage Walk, London.

Muhammad Ali was once beaten with a counter punch, of all places, in an aeroplane.

Asked by a stewardess to fasten his seatbelt, wisecracking Ali replied: 'Superman don't need a seatbelt.'

Quick as a flash the stewardess countered: 'Superman don't need an aeroplane – fasten your seatbelt!'

We all know Cassius Clay became Muhammad Ali with films and television ensuring that we also know Rocky Graziano started life as Rocco Bardella, but over the years many men have adopted an assumed ring name for various reasons. Joe Louis Barrow and Philip Scott Suffling took the easy route of simply dropping their last name. below are some of the better-known boxers who have made their nom-du-ring a household word in boxing circles.

Nom-du-ring	Real name	Nom-du-ring	Real name
Jack 'Kid' Berg	Judah Bergman	Dave Sands	David Richie
'Kid' Chocolate	Eligio Sardinas	Jack Dillon	Ernest Cutler Price
'Kid' McCoy	Norman Selby	Kid Gavilan	Gerado Gonzalez
Dixie Kid	Aaron Brown	Pete Herman	Peter Gullota
Ted 'Kid' Lewis	Gershon Mendeloff	Beau Jack	Sidney Walker
Battling Siki	Louis Phall	Stanley Ketchel	Stanislaus Kiecal
Battling Levinsky	Barney Lebrowitz	Lou Ambers	Louis D'Ambrosio
Battling Nelson	Oscar Neilsen	Jack Britton	William Breslin
Jack London	J G Harper	Mushy Callahan	Vincent Scheer
Jack Sharkey	John Coccoskey	Young Corbett II	William Rothwell
Philadelphia Jack O'Brien	Joseph Hagan	Jack Delaney	Ovila Chapdelaine
Tommy Ryan	Joseph Youngs	Dick Corbett	Richard Coleman
Tommy Burns	Noah Brusso	Tony Zale	Anthony Zaleski
Jock McAvoy	Joseph Bamford	Dick Tiger	Richard Ihetu
Ben Jeby	Morris Jebalowsky	Freddie Welsh	Fredrick Thomas
Jersey Joe Walcott	Arnold Cream	Hogan 'Kid' Bassey	Okon Bassey Asuquo
Sugar Ray Robinson	Walker Smith	Terry Allen	Edward Govier
Benny Leonard	Benjamin Leinert	Henry Armstrong	Henry Jackson
Willie Pep	William Papales	Pat Stribling	William Gardner
Barney Ross	Bernard Rosofsky	Sammy Angott	Samuel Engotti
Midget Wolgast	Joseph Lascalzo	Sal Bartolo	Salvatore Interbartolo
Small Montana	Benjamin Gan	Bermondsey Billy Wells	William Scroggins
Archie Moore	Archibald Wright	Eddie Mustfa Muhammad	Edward Gregory
Jack Root	Janos Ruthaly		

And here are some nicknames that, over the years, some boxers have acquired.

Nickname	Real name	Nickname	Real name
Louisville Lip	Cassius Clay	Fighting Marine	Gene Tunney
The Greatest	Muhammad Ali	Toy Bulldog	Mickey Walker
Peerless Jim	Jim Driscoll	Slapsie Maxie	Maxie Rosenbloom
Boston Strong Boy	John L Sullivan	Smokin' Joe	Joe Frazier
Ghost with a hammer in his hand	Jimmy Wilde	Whitechapel Whirlwind	Jack Kid Berg
Manassa Mauler	Jack Dempsey	Orchid Man	Georges Carpentier
The Algate Tiger	Al Phillips	Pattawatomie Giant	Jess Willard
Beer Barrel Palookas	Tony Galento	Black Ulan	Max Schemeling
Wild Bull of the Pampas	Louis Firpo	Human Windmill	Harry Greb
Little Chocolate	George Dixon	Little Artha	Jack Johnson
Homicide Hank	Henry Armstrong	Georgia Deacon	Tiger Flowers
Cinderella Man	James J Braddock	Hard Rock from Down Under	Tom Heeny
Kid Snowball	Ted Broadribb	Ageless Archie	Archie Moore
Rochdale thunderbolt	Jock McAvoy	Bronx Bull	Jake LaMotta
Phainting Phil	Phil Scott	Boston Gob	Jack Sharkey
Michigan Assassin	Stanley Ketchel	Non Pareil	Jack Dempsey
The Boilermaker	James J Jefferies	Casablanca Clouter	Marcel Cedan
Ruby Robert	Bob Fitzsimmons	Macho Man	Hector Comacho
Ambling Alp	Primo Carnera	Will O'the Wisp	Willie Pep
Clones Cyclone	Barry McGuigan	Terrible Tim	Tim Witherspoon
Brown Bomber	Joe Louis	Boom-Boom	Ray Mancini
The Game Chicken	Henry Pearce	Welsh Wizard	Freddie Welsh
Durable Dane	Battling Nelson	Madcap Maxie	Max Baer
Scotch Wop	Johnny Dundee	Boston Tar baby	Sam Langford
Boxing Bell-Hop	Fred Apostoli	The Hit Man	Thomas Hearns
Herkimer Hurricane	Lou Ambers	King of the Canebreaks	Young Stribling
Ghetto Wizard	Benny Leonard		

The Show Must Go On, is an old saying within the entertainment business but Control Board supremo Simon Block recalls the time the show, or more precisely, the main event almost didn't go on.

The date was June 25, 1988 and the main event was a proposed contest between Barry McGuigan and Thomas De Cruz. The venue was Luton Town Football Stadium.

Simon, in those days the Southern Area secretary, was on duty as BBBofC representative, when with only about two hours before the main event was scheduled for live television, he received a message from Lesley McCarthy of Frank Warren Promotions, that De Cruz was refusing to leave his hotel room. He was asked if he would go to the hotel and see what the problem was.

Simon says: 'In view of the fact that the roads around the stadium were packed with people and cars, I arranged for a police escort to take us to the hotel. In their room I found De Cruz's manager was being difficult about money. We started to negotiate but talking through an interpreter was slowing things down quite a lot and I realised that even if we did solve the problem we were going to be too late to get back to the venue in time for the live transmission. Therefore I persuaded them to continue discussions back at the stadium.

We all got into the lift, De Cruz, his manager, trainer, the lady interpreter, two policemen, Mr McCarthy and myself, making eight in all. At the ground floor the lift overshot and the doors jammed shut. The hotel staff couldn't get them open so, in desperation, I asked one of the policemen to call the Fire Brigade on his portable 'phone. By the time they arrived and set us free we had been stuck for about half an hour.

It soon became clear that De Cruz's manager suffered from claustrophobia and after about ten minutes he started acting rather strangely. He was sweating quite profusely and began taking his clothes off ending up stripped to the waist.

When we finally got out a police car was waiting for us and with sirens blasting forth and driving on the wrong side of the road – the other side being a solid mass of traffic – we got to the stadium with just over half an hour to spare. The manager was so relived to be out of that lift that all argument had gone out of him and the bout went on as planned, with McGuigan winning in the fourth round.

No-one of the press or among the twelve thousand strong crowd had any idea of how close it had come to being called off altogether.'

Joe Louis

In the heavyweight world championship race, The Brown Bomber Joe Louis stands in a class of his own as far as world records stand.

He took part in the most championship bouts – 27 in all, which is a record in itself; he won 26 of those bouts, which is another record; he won his 26 championship bouts consecutively, yet another record and he holds the record for the most championship bouts won by the KO route, which is 22. He also holds the record of 5 one round KOs in championship bouts.

But for winning on a disqualification against Buddy Baer on January 9, 1942, Joe would have the record for the most consecutive championship bouts won by KO. But as Baer spoilt that record of 14 Louis settled for second best with 7 consecutive KOs. But, to demonstrate what could have been, this feat he achieved TWICE.

In a career as world heavyweight champion, which started on June 22, 1937 when he took the title from James J Braddock by an eighth round KO, right up until he was deposed by Ezzard Charles on September 27, 1950 on points over 15 rounds. Joe only travelled the distance on four occasions.

In addition to Charles, the others managing to stay on their feet for the final bell were Tommy Farr (August 30, 1937) in Yankee Stadium, Bronx, New York, Arturo Godoy (February 9, 1940) and Jersey Joe Walcott (December 5, 1947) both in Madison Square Gardens, New York.

Despite going the full distance on those four occasions and with Abe Simon (March 21, 1941) and Billy Conn (June 18, 1941) lasting 13 rounds, with Bob Pastor (September 20, 1941) and Jersey Joe (June 25, 1948) hanging around for 11 rounds apiece, Joe Louis only fought 120 rounds in his 27 championship winning bouts – and that must be yet another record.

When Welshman Tommy Farr fought Joe Louis for the heavyweight championship of the world, at Yankee Stadium New York, on August 30, 1937, their contest created two records.

It was only 77 days since Louis had won the title by stopping James J Braddock in the eighth round, in Chicago and the quickest that any heavyweight world champion had defended his title to date.

As both boxers were 23, they were the youngest ever contestants for heavyweight world honours up to that time.

Joe Louis started his professional career with a KO when he knocked out Jack Kracken in 1934. Nineteen years later his career ended in the same way – but this time it was Joe that suffered the KO, when Rocky Marciano stopped him on October 26, 1951.

In between Joe had inflicted KOs on 54 opponents, including eight men that had held the world crown. They were: Carnera, Baer, Schmeling, Sharkey, Braddock, Lewis, Conn and Walcott.

JOE LOUIS
HEAVYWEIGHT CHAMPION of the WORLD

These days Simon Block is head honcho at the British Boxing Board of Control but a few years back he 'did a bit' himself. He well remembers his first bout, as a fifteen year old with the Crawley Amateur Boxing Club.

He recalls: 'My first sparring session was with a young lad who was a couple of years older than me but he was so fast I couldn't see the punches coming and I was reduced to covering up to save myself. After the session I protested to my dad that this chap was too fast for me and always seemed to be one jump ahead. Dad brushed aside my arguments telling me that I would become a fine boxer and much better than my erstwhile opponent.

Although my dad had a good knowledge of boxing and was a good boxer himself in his day, on this occasion I think he got it wrong – that other fellow was Alan Minter.'

Sugar Ray Leonard noticed the family of Bruce Finch crying at the ringside after their 1981 clash.

In an interview he said: 'I felt bad. His wife was crying; his kids were crying. But then if I had lost my wife would have been crying and my kids would have been crying.'

Asked by the interviewer: 'Does it make you wonder about boxing as a sport when it makes people cry?'

Leonard replied: 'No. Unemployment makes you cry.'

An old saying within boxing circles tells us an illiterate boxer may sign with a cross and a manager of dubious credentials may well use a double cross.

Peter Ford has the distinction of being beaten by former British middleweight champion Albert Finch – twice in the same day.

Peter ran a seafood stall in Croydon and one day Finch asked for a large order. When the order was ready Finch dropped the bombshell: 'I don't like paying cash.'

Peter could see his profits disappearing as Finch was getting ready to leave without paying but the former champ was no freeloader and he told Peter: ' I have a package of meat here that I will exchange for the seafood.'

Having agreed to the swop, Ford was still the loser because the meat turned out to be pork chops and being of the Jewish faith he was not able to eat the meat and was obliged to give it away.

The fight of the long count will always be remembered as the one in Chicago when Jack Dempsey put Gene Tunney down for what transpired as 14 seconds, on September 22, 1927.

But a similar thing that has almost been overlooked, happened far more recently when Mike Tyson decked Buster Douglas in the eighth round of their scheduled twelve rounder world championship bout in Tokyo, Japan on February 11, 1990.

Tyson had Douglas down and due to some confusion the referee didn't take up the count straight away, allowing Douglas at least three extra seconds to struggle to his feet, at which time he was saved by the bell.

It was costly blunder on the part of the referee, because two round later Douglas turned the tables and knocked out Tyson.

After the tragedy which cost him the world crown, Tyson said: 'I've lost before, I can handle losing but I want to lose fairly.'

Referee Octavio Meyran, the man who cost Tyson the title, conceded: 'Rules are rules. I accept that I made a mistake.'

When Terry Allen turned professional on September 3, 1942, at the age of 18 he had behind him a formidable amateur career of winning all but five of his 107 amateur bouts.

The betting was 4–1 for John L Sullivan when he was matched against James J Corbett for the world heavyweight crown, in New Orleans on September 7, 1892.

Corbett, the challenger, defeated the old champion by a KO in the 21st round.

The odds were the same when Corbett, as new champion, met Bob Fitzsimmons in Carson City on March 17, 1897 – and again the challenger KO'd the reigning champion.

In both cases the challenger was the lighter man.

When Corbett beat Sullivan he weighed 178 pounds against Sullivans 212 pounds. Then Corbett, in turn, was deposed by a lighter Fitzsimmons. Fitz scaled 167 pounds against Corbetts 183 pounds.

Jersey Joe Walcott suffered double trouble when he was on the losing end of world championship bouts six times. He lost twice to Joe Louis, twice to Ezzard Charles and twice to Rocky Marciano.

Professor Andy Newton is reputed to have had 558 contests and only lost the decision on 43 occasions.

Wayne McCullough, Northern Ireland's only Gold Medalist in the 1990 Commonwealth Games, had his own personal party at the medal ceremony.

When he mounted the rostrum to receive his medal for winning the light flyweight division, the tape of the anthem The Londonderry Air – better known as Danny Boy – wouldn't work so an official got up and sang it and the audience joined in.

Sugar Ray Leonard was christened Ray Charles Leonard because his mother hoped he would be a singer.

He had his first bout when he was about seven years old and it made him feel so bad that he vowed never to box again. However, he did try again and this time progressed through to the 1972 Olympic selection competition where he suffered a defeat the semi-final stage. Along the way he had lied about his age: he was only fifteen.

Four years later he not only qualified but also won a Gold Medal.

When he turned professional Leonard received $50,000 for his first fight. By contrast one of his toughest opponents, Marvin Haglar, only got $50 for his first pro fight.

Throughout his boxing career Leonard is said to have earned in excess of sixty million dollars.

In an interview he said: 'I didn't know there was so much money to be made in the sport of boxing. After all my actual boxing was only about five years.' (he had a couple of periods of fairly long inactivity)

Centurion Ray Fallone may have been a high flyer in the ring but it was a different story in the air.

He recalled: 'My first time in a 'plane was on a trip to Ireland where I was booked to fight Chris McAuley at the Ulster Hall, Belfast. It was one of those old propeller type aircraft and I was so frightened that by the time we landed I had lost about seven pounds through fear.

Before the weigh-in my manager made me drink two and a half pints of Guinness.'

Bob Fitzsimmons won the middleweight title by knocking out champion Jack Dempsey (The Nonpareil) on January 4, 1891, in New Orleans.

He then defended his new title by knocking out two more challengers, in March 1893 and September 1894. Then he turned his attention to the heavyweight division where he took the heavyweight crown from James J Corbett, on March 17, 1897.

When the light heavyweight division was formed in 1903, Bob challenged George Gardner, the new division champion and, on November 25, 1903 became the new light heavyweight champion.

This third title win made Bob Fitzsimmons the first man to win world titles at three different weights – and this despite Bob never weighing much more than twelve stones and four pounds.

The 1908 Olympic Games, held in London, British boxers took every medal in all three classes, Gold, Silver and Bronze – except one.

The man to spoil the clean sweep was middleweight Reggie Baker who, boxing for Australasia, took a Silver.

Forty years later and again in London, the situation was almost a complete reversal but with two British boxers winning a Silver apiece.

Johnny Wright mirrored Baker's Silver win at middleweight and Don Scott put the cherry on the cake by mounting the Silver rostrum spot, at light heavyweight.

Jack Woodman, father of Southern Area light heavyweight champ, Ernie Woodman, decided to name his sons after the biblical disciples – Matthew, Mark etc.

But why Ernie of all things?

Ernie said: 'There were twelve disciples and by the time it was my turn he had run out of names, because there were nineteen boys in my family.'

An Englishman and a Frenchman were going at it hammer and tongs in a Paris ring, in the early 1930s with the Frenchman finally going down.

The Englishman leaned over the prostate body and snarled: 'Stay where you are. If you get up I'll knock you out.'

The referee quickly advised him to desist with the taunts, which brought the instant witty reply: 'So what, he doesn't understand English anyway.'

Old time fighters certainly had fantastic staying power and that was demonstrated on June 3, 1889, when Fred Brogan fought Del Hawkins for a full seventy five rounds. As no decision was arrived at, they continued the bout on the following day until Brogan knocked out Hawkins in the fifteenth round – making a total of NINETY rounds of fighting.

Referees

Leading British referee Harry Gibbs was suffering from a bad throat as he arrived to take charge of his part of the bill, as third man, at Bristol. Then, to complicate matters, the second referee failed to turn up leaving Harry to officiate on the entire programme.

His voice got steadily worse as the night progressed until the bout between his namesake, Lenny Gibbs and Danny Please, when it failed completely.

Harry remembers: 'By the time I got to the Gibbs v Please bout I had lost my voice altogether and I refereed their entire contest without saying a word.'

Paddy Sower, referee of Wembley Arena and National Sporting Club fame, had a similar 'mute' experience at the Royal Albert Hall, but for different reasons.

He said; 'It was a humble undercard six rounder between Jimmy Bott and Dave Smith. It was in the third round that I suddenly realised that I hadn't spoken to either boxer and, at the end of the six rounds I still hadn't spoken a word to them. Credit to both boxers for their part in what was the best and cleanest contest that I ever refereed.'

Old campaigner turned referee, Benny Caplan didn't believe in touching the boxers more than absolutely necessary. He said: 'I never used to get involved in pulling them apart. I would tell them to break and expect them to do so.'

He didn't believe in saying a lot either. Three bouts under his control as third man went by without a word being spoken – and one of those bouts was a title contest from the National Sporting Club.

Harry Gibbs had a long and distinguished career as Britians leading referee and his achievements were recognised with the award of an OBE for his services to boxing. But Harry remembers his first refereeing job, which was a long way from the acclaim he received in later years.

As a young lance corporal with the Queens Royal Regiment, he was taken prisoner of war and incarcerated at the Stalzenberg Lager work camp, Marienburg. Having been an amateur boxer prior to his army service, Harry soon had some training exercises organised and, although weak through lack of proper food, they even managed some light sparring.

Another soldier in the prison camp was Bill Warner. Harry asked Bill if he did any boxing. Bill replied: 'No not much but I am a professional wrestler and I hold the Southern Area Championship.'

Harry invited Bill to help with the training programme and they soon had a wrestling match arranged against a French wrestler, who was also a prisoner.

Harry Gibbs refereed the match and he recalled: 'That was my first refereeing job.'

After army service during World War II, Harry Gibbs became instructor to the English ABA boxing team, based at St Pancras gym, London.

One day in the early 1950s heavyweight Billy Walkers sparring partner failed to arrive and Harry had to spar in his place.

Boxing correspondent Charles Darby was watching and advised Harry to give up boxing and go for refereeing instead, saying: 'You're getting too old for this.'

Harry took the advice and applied to take the referees exam – and passed with flying colours.

He said: 'Only two of us passed the tough exam and the other chap retired soon after, which left me the only one. I went from Class B to Class A and on to Class A Star in only four years. That was a record then and I think it still stands today. I'm very proud of that achievement.'

Willie Pastrano was getting a real beating in New York when, at the end of a round, the referee came over to his corner and asked: 'Pastrano, where are you?'

Wisecracking Willie replied: 'I'm in Madison Square Gardens having the shit kicked out of me.'

The bout continued.

May 18, 1948 Laurie Buxton took a points verdict over Mike DeCosmo but had to raise his own hand in a victory salute because the referee had caught the last punch of the contest and was out cold.

Benny Caplan (L) v Jack Corbett (R)
February 12, 1940
Empress Hall, Earls Court

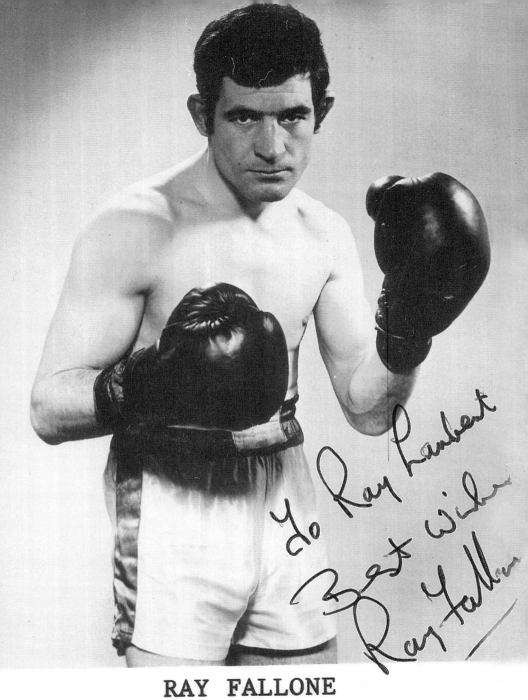

RAY FALLONE
LAST-CENTURIAN 100-PRO FIGHTS
BATTERSEA

A Star referee Larry O'Connell, the third man in the ring on many televised boxing shows, had a far from glorious start to his refereeing career – he was booed out of the ring.

It was at the Anglo-American Sporting Club on February 23, 1976. Larry gave an unpopular decision but he said: 'I didn't let the booing upset me. I came straight back and refereed another bout,' – and the rest, as they say, is history.

Jersey Joe Walcott defended his world heavyweight title in June 1952 against Ezzard Charles – the man that he took the championship from a year earlier.

On that historic occasion the third man in the ring was Zack Clayton. Thus making it an all black affair and the first time that a black referee had officiated at a world heavyweight title fight.

When Roberto Gonzalez stopped a very low blow in his bout against Jamie Castillo, during the summer of 1990, he was obviously unable to continue. So it was left to the referee to sort out the confusion, which he eventually did by declaring a no contest, thereby saving face for both boxers and avoiding a possible riot among the spectators.

As luck would have it that referee was the best possible man for the task, his name was, of all things, John Thomas!

The Harry Wills v Jack Thompson bout, in 1921, was such a non-event with both boxers not trying that referee Eddie Hanlon showed his contempt by walking out of the ring, He refused to return and would not give a decision.

On June 17, 1972, Britians best remembered referee Harry Gibbs was in charge of the world title clash when Jean Claude Bouttier challenged Carlos Monzon for his middleweight crown, in Paris.

In the twelfth Monzon caught Bouttier with a splendid shot that had Bouttier heading for the canvas but in the heat of the moment Monzon leapt forward to get in another blow before his opponent hit the deck.

Referee Harry, spotting the potential dangers of such a manoeuvre, quickly stepped forward catching Bouttier in his arms, preventing him from crashing heavily. At the same time Harry raised his free arm to ward off Monzon and in so doing accidentally brushed Monzon lightly on his nose; for reasons best known only to himself, Monzon pretended he was hurt and staggered about all over the ring.

Harry Gibbs recalled: 'It was only a very light touch on his nose and he was obviously acting hurt but just for a second I had the thought that if he goes down I shall be left with a double knockout.'

As it transpired Monzon was only skylarking and all ended well with him retaining his title.

But referee Gibbs had the last word: 'Just as well he stopped playing about because if he had gone down I would have had no alternative but to disqualify him.'

~ 🜊 ~

Moss DeYong, the well known referee of the 1940s and 1950s, allowed his usual stern facial expression to relax for once as he indicated Billy Boot and Harry Legge to their respective corners prior to their bout in Cambridge in 1946.

DeYong couldn't help a broad grin as he realised the connection between LEGGE and BOOT.

~ 🜊 ~

When Ad Wolgast defended his world lightweight crown against Joe Rivers, on July 4, 1912, both boxers threw punches at the very same moment and both were felled – but for some reason the referee picked up Wolgast and supported him on his feet whilst counting out Rivers

~ 🜊 ~

Just prior to World War II the Pullum Promotions used to pick up their boxers in London and transport them to Oxford Town Hall shows by coach.

On one such occasion with the two promoters WA (Bill) Pullum, WS (Young Billy) Pullum and the boxers, was referee Mickey Fox.

During the journey they were discussing one of the opponents on that nights bill, a Scotsman named George Dower. The dialogue went like this:

'How is George?'

'He's OK except that he entered a beauty contest,' said referee Fox.

'How did he fare?'

'Very unlucky. He came second,' replied Fox. 'A horse won it!'

There are several stories about boxers being concussed in the ring and somehow managing to finish their bout and occasionally coming out the winner – by remote control. Sometimes they 'come-to' in the shower, sometimes it is on the way home later that night and, almost unbelievably, sometimes not until the following day. But, strange as it may seem, during the intervening period they have acted perfectly normal with people close by noticing nothing unusual in their behaviour.

Harry Legge, Bournemouth lightweight and booth fighter of note during the 1940s and 1950s recalls such an experience.

He was boxing Laurie Buxton in 1949, at Bournemouth Town Hall in front of his hometown fans, when he went down from what he described as a light punch. Scrambling to his feet, he was just in time to see the referee raise his opponents hand as the winner.

Feeling outraged at his unjust dismissal, Harry danced around the ring shadow boxing like a man possessed to show that he was not hurt but to no avail. The referee had made his decision and it stood.

Upon leaving the ring Harry asked his second for his views on his diabolical dismissal.

'Well Harry, you were down four times in quick succession, you know. You were slipping about all over the place and you seemed unable to keep your feet,' was the frank answer.

Decades later Harry still had no recollection of those earlier knockdowns.

Irish heavyweight Jack Doyle was pitted against Eddie Phillips on an open air show at White City in 1938. At ringside was a crowd of spectators who had put a lot of money on Phillips to win at very favourable odds.

Suddenly their prayers were answered. The Irish Nightingale stopped a powerful right-hander that knocked him right out of the ring.

In his dazed state Doyle tried to rise but found that he was unable to do so. The gamblers, seeing a heaven sent opportunity, prevented him from getting up by standing on his wrists.

He was duly counted out and a lot of money was won by a gaggle of delighted spectators.

For years after Jack Doyle admitted he had taken a first class crack on the jaw but he was at a loss to understand why both of his wrists were sore for several days after that bout.

37

Jack Turner, the man who discovered and trained Freddie Mills, also worked on fairground booths as a speiler – the man on the mike. So it was probably through this side of his business that he was known as the man that was never lost for words – except once!

Jack also ran a very busy boxing stable in the 1940s and his boxers were in action in venues as far apart as Penzance and Edinburgh. It was while travelling with his stable that the historic occasion when Jack ran out of words occurred.

The show was at Tredgar and Jacks lads comprised half of the bill. They arrived at Tredgar late in the afternoon after a long and tiring journey across the Welsh valleys by train, bus and coach, from their Bournemouth base.

The coach unloaded them into the High Street and a passer-by was asked for directions to the venue for that nights show. 'I dunno about any boxing tonight,' he told them, 'but there is a professional bill here in a weeks time. I reckon you got here a week too early.'

The hungry, weary and now disillusioned boxers turned on their manager and Jack spluttered, turned a nice shade of red and finally dived into his pocket for the confirmatory letter. Yes, the show was next week!

Jack made the excuse that they kept him so busy that sometimes something had to go wrong and this was one of those times. This, they knew, was true enough and worse things happen at sea (and in the ring) but never the less, it was a lame excuse and they all knew it. For an hour or so after Mr Jack Turner, the eloquent spieler was completely at a loss for words.

Harry Legge was one of the party on that historic day and he recalled that for a long time the mere mention of Tredgar was enough to send their manager into a fit of depression.

Gene Tunney and Rocky Marciano share more in common that the heavyweight world title. They both won the coveted crown on the same date: September 23. Tunney in 1926 and Marciano in 1952.

By further co-incidence both title winning bouts took place in Philadelphia

Tunney beat Jack Dempsey over ten rounds in the Sesquicentennial Stadium and Marciano KO'd Jersey Joe Walcott in the thirteenth of a fifteen rounder at the Municipal Stadium.

James J Jeffries is the only heavyweight world champion to have won a championship bout in less than one minute. This was on April 6, 1900. He knocked out Jack Finnegan in fifty-five seconds, in the Detroit Armoury, Michigan.

Now for one of those 'Irish' stories:

One of Britain's best remembered world champions, who insists upon remaining anonymous, relates this tale about his second who on this occasion just happened to be Irish.

He says: 'We were boxing in a large open-air arena and the dressing rooms were way down below, along endless tunnels. My second and I came to the ring after what seemed like an eternity of walking along those tunnels and then across the grass then, as I went to glove up I noticed that he was trying to put my hand in the wrong glove.

'On closer inspection I found that he had brought out two left gloves; he just had to be Irish. Then everybody had to wait while he went all the way back to get a different pair.'

The anonymous boxer vows this is a true story.

And another:

Billy Conn challenged Joe Louis for the world title in the Polo Grounds, New York, on Wednesday June 18, 1941.

By the third round Conn was creeping ahead and fighting back so hard that Louis was forced to hold on to save himself; a rare thing for Louis to do.

He kept up the barrage for the entire fourth round and renewed his attack during the eighth and again during the twelfth, when it looked like he had Louis at his mercy.

But instead of listening to advice from his seconds and staying away, Conn charged in like an enraged bull to clinch victory in the thirteenth. But Louis retaliated and rattled a tattoo of punches to the head and Conn was down and counted out, with only a few seconds of the round remaining.

Later Billy Conn was told that not following advice had cost him the world championship. The wisecracking Irishman is alleged to have replied: 'What's the use of me being Irish if I can't be thick.'

A Manchester hotel decided to hold a boxing show but so cramped were their surroundings that there was no space for changing rooms. So the local Fire Brigade, always ready to lend a helping hand, stepped in with an offer for the contestants to use their showers and facilities.

This offer was gratefully accepted by the boxers even though it meant that the dressing rooms were quite a way from the ring – about two miles in fact.

Ray Fallone, Britain's last centurion (100 pro bouts to his credit) was on that bill and he remembered: 'The hotel was way out in the sticks and we had to change in the Fire Station and travel to the venue in our boxing kit, in the back of the fire-fighters van.'

Servicemen

The salty tales flowed when London promoter Ronnie Ezra and Scottish promoter Sammy Docherty met at the Empress Hall, London on October 10, 1950.

They had both served on the same ship during World War II. Ezra as a seaman and Docherty as a stoker – but neither knew the other was a boxing promoter.

Fancy learning that you are dead from the pages of a magazine!

That is what happened to Imperial Services champion, Harry Nicholls. Harry did the double in 1938 by winning the heavyweight championship of the army and the Imperial Services Championship.

On May 21, 1940 lance corporal Nicholls platoon was in Belgium and were sent forward under heavy fire to silence some enemy gun posts, suffering severe casualties as they did so until only Harry was left standing. Although wounded at least four times himself, he carried on alone and destroyed three machine gun nests before collapsing and being taken prisoner.

Harry Nicholls was awarded a Victoria Cross for his bravery.

Whilst in the POW hospital he was reported killed in action and his Victoria Cross was presented to his wife by King George VI at Buckingham Palace, on August 6, 1940.

When Harry was recovered from his injuries and transferred to a prison camp, one of the first things he saw was a copy of Picture Post magazine and inside was a picture of his wife and baby receiving his posthumous medal from the King.

Harry was repatriated in 1945 and his medal was returned to the King who decorated Harry at the Palace on June 22, 1945.

As well as his boxing double, Harry Nicholls has the distinction of being the first man to win the Victoria Cross in World War II and is believed to be the only case in history of the coveted award where the same medal has been presented twice.

The Royal Navy's aircraft carrier HMS Illustrious mounted an historic event on March 24, 1994, when the navy boys challenged officer cadets from Sandhurst Military Academy to a six man boxing tournament.

As befitting such an occasion, there were no losers and with each team producing three winners, the result of a first class contest afloat was a 3–3 draw.

As a prisoner of war, in Marienburg, Germany during World War II, Harry Gibbs, later to become Britans top referee, fought a three one minute round bout with fellow soldier 'Cleats' MacKenzie.

Harry recalled bitterly: 'A couple of days later Cleats was dead – murdered by the German guards. They shot him.'

Boxing for the RAF in the European championships of 1953 in Warsaw, Bruce Wells was so happy to have won through to the final of his weight class, that he gave his Gold Medal to the team coach.

On June 20, 1942 30,000 fans witnessed an all Royal Air Force boxing show at Tottenham Football ground.

Sergeant Freddie Mills beat Pilot Officer Len Harvey, for the British and European light heavyweight titles.

The referee was corporal Eugene Henderson and the promoter was air-craftsman John Muldoon.

Mills did his final training for the bout at the appropriately named 'The Airman' pub, in Middlesex.

Mills 22, had Harvey 34, down for eight in the second round and as he got up he was knocked clear out of the ring and failed to beat the count.

The whole thing was over in less than four minutes.

Norman Duff, British boxer of the early 1950s, received his call-up papers to join the RAF for National Service but unfortunately for him, the date the military required his services was the very day that boxing also required his services. He was booked to make his professional debut that very evening.

Norman got over the problem by simply sending a telegram stating, 'Sorry but I am making my professional boxing debut on that day.'

The authorities gave him the OK to go ahead and allowed him a couple of more days after, presumably in case he needed the time to recuperate.

~ 🕯 ~

It is not very well known that light heavyweight champion Freddie Mills, who was to go on to world honours, actually appeared in the ring with heavyweight champions Joe Louis and Jack Dempsey in 1944.

During World War II Joe Louis was in England with an American army boxing team, doing exhibitions around the American service bases. For one such bout against fellow American George Nicholson, Mills was asked to referee.

Then, a couple of weeks later, at another exhibition and again on an American base, Freddie Mills was invited to box American sergeant Bob Scully and he was thrilled when the referee was introduced as Jack Dempsey.

So it can truthfully be said that Mills had been in the ring with two of the greatest heavyweight champions of all time.

~ 🕯 ~

London flyweight, Terry Allen, who went on to world honours on April 25, 1950, changed his name to Terry Allen in memory of a pal who died whilst serving with the Royal Navy during World War II. Terry, who also served in the navy during the war, started life as Edward Govier.

~ 🕯 ~

Theo Medina, the French bantamweight, won the Croix de Guerre during World War II and was presented his award by Charles De Gaulle.

~ 🕯 ~

'Seaman' Bill Storrie, navy middleweight boxer of the 1930s was just about one step away from a shot at the British championship, which he was almost certain to have won when the Royal Navy 'requested' that he retired from all boxing.

Bill, Inter Services middleweight champion in 1933 and also RN and RM middleweight champion the same year, had just qualified as a naval gunnery instructor and the reasoning behind the request was that any damage to his eyes and the navy would lose a valuable asset.

Len Harvey

HEAVYWEIGHT CHAMPION.

LEN HARVEY, CRUISER WEIGHT CHAMPION OF GREAT BRITAIN AND WINNER OUTRIGHT OF THE LONSDALE MIDDLEWEIGHT CHAMPIONSHIP BELT.

Norman Duff

His manager, WS 'Young Billy' Pullum was invited to a meeting with the navy top brass at Chatham where they asked that, as manager, he persuade Bill to give up boxing completely to allow him to concentrate on his career with the Senior Service.

Bill complied and was soon in action when World War II came along.

He was taken prisoner of war but escaped to Alexandria where he went along to watch a boxing show. His shipmates there asked him to enter an 'open' competition because they had no beer money. Bill obliged and won the competition.

Bill went on to complete 44 years service, the latter part with the Australian Navy. He retired as a lieutenant commander.

George Jones was obliged to change his name through some military regulation. With hundreds if not thousands of service boxers at the time, it's hard to fathom what that obscure regulation was – or why they just picked on George.

However, George complied and changed to Jack O'Dare and, as Jack O'Dare, went on to a successful career, along the way becoming a firm favourite at The Ring, Blackfriars, where he boxed regularly.

At an age when most boxers are thinking of retiring, ex-sailor Johnny Buff quit the navy and turned pro, at the age of thirty.

Three years later his faith in himself was justified and he became welterweight world champion, taking the title, in New Orleans from little tough guy, Pete Herman.

~ 🌴 ~

Stoker Tim Cole, the navy's fighting welterweight, fought his way through to the 1942 finals of the Golden Gloves tournament, held in Vancouver, while his ship was in the nearby Navy Yards. The tournament promoters did him proud and gave the fighting stoker his dressing gown and shorts in addition to his runner-up trophy, at the competition end.

Tim stowed his mementos in his locker back on board and later, when his ship, HMS York, was off Greece it was dive-bombed and sunk. The very first bomb scored a direct hit on his locker and all his possessions were lost.

The fighting Stoker survived although his kit and trophies didn't. Many years later, Tim became the chairman of Kent Ex-Boxers Association

Joey Archibald featherweight world champion of the late 1930s, saw the writing on the wall when he lost all but four of his last thirty bouts. Although a veteran of more than 100 contests, he decided that he might have more luck in a different kind of fighting so, in 1943 he retired from the ring and joined the navy.

Willie Pep, well-remembered world featherweight champ of the 1940s, liked military life so much that when he was discharged from the American navy after service in World War II, he promptly re-enlisted – this time with the army.

Johnny King, owner of two Lonsdale belts won outright at bantamweight, was a navy man aboard HMS Prince of Wales when Japanese dive bombers sank her during World War II.

Johnny had to swim and luckily he survived to continue his boxing career after his discharge at the wars end.

'Seaman' Ernie Noble, Chatham sailor and former amateur, won a novices heavyweight competition at Crystal Palace on August Bank Holiday 1937, beating Pat Burke in the final.

Ernie KO'd Burke in the second round but for reasons best known to himself, the referee ordered them to box on so Ernie repeated the feat for a second time before the end of the round.

'Seaman' Tommy Watson was a Chatham based sailor who set up his training camp in 'The Monarch' pub not far from the dockyard gate. Tommy had 115 bouts (1927-1935) and won 105 of them. He took the British featherweight title from Nel Tarleton at Liverpool Stadium on November 10, 1932 and, riding on a crest of success, challenged 'Kid' Chocolate for the world championship, in New York, on March 19 the following year. Tommy held Chocolate for the full fifteen rounds but just failed to get the verdict.

There have been eighteen first round knockouts in heavyweight world championship bouts to date, including James J Jefferies 55 seconds record KO of Jack Finnegan on April 6, 1900.

Joe Louis being the most successful exponent. Louis achieved the feat an incredible five times. His luckless opponents were:

        Max Schemeling June 22, 1938

        John Henry Lewis January 25, 1939

        Jack Roper April 17, 1939

        Buddy Baer Jan 9, 1942

        Tami Mauriello September 18 1946

Sonny Liston reached the list of double KO champions by twice knocking out Floyd Patterson in the first round, on September 25, 1962 and again on July 22, 1963. But then he had the misfortune of suffering a first round KO himself at the hands of Muhammad Ali on May 25, 1965.

The only other heavyweight world champion to join the doubles club is Tommy Burns. Tommy knocked out Bill Squires on July 4, 1907 and repeated the feat on Jem Roache on March 17, 1908.

Other first round KOs are as follows:

        Rocky Marciano v Jersey Joe Walcott May 15, 1953

        Joe Frazier v Dave Zyglewicz April 22, 1969

        George Foreman v Jose Ramon September 1, 1973

        Michael Dokes v Mike Weaver December 8, 1982

        Larry Holmes v Marvis Frazier November 25, 1983

        James Smith v Tim Witherspoon December 12, 1986

        Mike Tyson v Michael Spinks June 27, 1988

Captain Robert Nairac, of the SAS Regiment, was a very keen amateur boxer before his untimely death whilst on duty in Northern Ireland.

During his undergraduate days at Oxford he is credited with saving the Oxford University Boxing Club. The club was on the verge of closing down when Robert managed to find enough people to form a team to face Cambridge University.

His makeshift team lost 5–4 that year but the following year they reversed that decision by winning by the same margin.

By his one-man 'whip' Robert Nairac saved his university boxing club from extinction.

Chatham Jack Edwards, the well known boxing trainer during the heyday of such popular boxing venues as Rochester Casino and the The Ring, Blackfriars, mainly between the wars, had a trick up his sleeve that usually brought tears to the eyes of his boxers opponents.

Before a particularly tough fight, 'Chatham Jack' would try to give his man an advantage by smearing him in wintergreen ointment, a particular foul smelling old fashioned medication.

His boxer would then be instructed to keep his dressing gown on until the very last second then, at the bell, whip it off quickly and go into a clinch.

The smell of the unpleasant aroma was usually enough to take the opponents breath way, allowing Jack's man to land several telling blows unopposed.

Pat Floyd was one of England's best ever amateur champions. He was ABA heavyweight champion in 1929, 1934, 1935 and again in 1946. As well as being a first class champion Pat was also a true amateur and always refused to accept payment for what he considered his sport.

In 1929 Pat boxed a three round exhibition with British Empire heavyweight champion Phil Scott, with the proceeds going to a charity.

In 1935 Pat won the Golden Gloves championship in New York, which in effect, made him, unofficially, the world amateur heavyweight champion. Former Heavyweight world champ, Gene Tunney, refereed that contest and Gene tried to persuade Pat to turn professional but Pat would not be budged and insisted upon remaining true to his amateur status.

After a very successful ring career, Pat became a professional referee but still refused to accept any payment from the sport he loved. He donated all his refereeing fees to the Control Board Benevolent Fund.

Pat Floyd was probably the only true amateur we have ever had.

By contrast and almost sixty years on:

After his bout in the 2008 ABA Finals, middleweight George Groves, who said that he had been training four days a week, told the interviewer something along the lines of .... if the ABA gives us enough money to live on and to feed the family ....

What money? Whatever happened to amateur?

Two managers talking:

No 1: 'I can't fight you at that weight.'

No 2: 'Alright, I'll fight you with my other lad.'

Who are they trying to kid.

June 25, 1952 was one of the hottest days that New York had ever seen. The temperature was 104 degrees in Yankee Stadium when Sugar Ray Robinson challenged Joey Maxim for the world light heavyweight title.

The bout was a real sizzler but it was the heat that stole the show.

At the end of the tenth round referee ruby Goldstein was overcome by the heat and was replaced by new referee Ray Miller. Then, three rounds later, Robinson staggered back to his corner completely exhausted and was unable to continue leaving Maxim, who was well behind on points, to retain his title by a TKO. This was the first time that Robinson had ever been stopped.

July 4, 1919 in Toledo, Ohio, boxing recognised women as spectators for the first time by setting aside a special enclosure for them. 2,000 women took advantage of this policy turnaround to watch Jack Dempsey become the new heavyweight champion of the world.

Lionel Rose, Australian welterweight was an Aborigine.

Dave Sands, Australian middleweight was an Aborigine.

Earl Wallis, Canadian heavyweight was Cherokee Indian.

Joe Louis, long time world heavyweight champion, was part Cherokee Indian.

The first 'Battle of the Century' took place on July 4, 1910, in Reno, Nevada when James J Jefferies was called out of retirement to put a stop to Jack Johnson's championship run.

Things didn't quite go according to plan and big Jim was counted out in the fifteenth round of a scheduled 45 rounder. He was floored three times in his last round – the first time he had ever been off his feet.

15,760 fans packed into the purpose built 20,000 seat arena to watch Johnson earn 120,000 dollars for the destruction of the big white hope.

Although he knew that he had been in a fight, Jefferies slipped back into retirement with 170,000 dollars in his pocket.

How times change:

In the 1870s, Tom Anderson, who later was to become the ABA president (1887 – 1893) was disqualified in one of his bouts under the Queensbury Rules, for fighting.

Three quarters of a century later, Ingemar Johansson, who would later find fame as professional world heavyweight champion, was disqualified in the final of the 1952 Olympic Games in Helsinki, for not trying.

Yes, how times change.

The first open air stadium specially built for boxing in Carson City, saw Englishman Bob Fitzsimmons beat James J Corbett for the world championship but very few people witnessed the bout and the purpose built stands were almost empty.

However, this bout on March 17, 1897 was filmed and the film of this historic occasion is reported to have made more money that all previous world championships added together.

Every sport has its cowboys but boxing can boast of the real thing, Bat Masterton, marshall of Dodge City was timekeeper for the Jake Kilrain v John L Sullivan bout in 1889.

Then, a few years later, Wyatt Earp, of OK Corral fame, refereed a Fitzsimmons v Sharkey bout held in San Francisco, in December 1896. Earp, possibly still revelling in a reputation built five years earlier, entered the ring with a gun in his belt.

But Fitzsimmons was not intimidated and in the eighth round laid the local hero low with a solar plexus blow that four decades later Jim Lawlor would turn into an art form.

The famous Wyatt Earp didn't know what to do, so, to save a riot and possible personal injury from all the Sharkey fans, he awarded the bout to Sharkey who was still on the deck.

Henry Cooper, former British heavyweight champion, holds the record number of three Lonsdale Belts won outright. However, his record will never be beaten because the practice of awarding another Belt for every successive third defence had been abandoned

Nowadays, just one Belt, immaterial of how many wins/defences are achieved, has been adopted – after the usual three notches have been acquired of course.

Clever Dicks

When gum shields were first talked about in England, having been an American new invention, Battersea heavyweight Ernie Woodman decided to make one of his own. He tried out many different compounds without much luck until he hit upon Gutta Persia, a tough kind of resin that set hard as rock. Unfortunately there was no give in it and the first time he was hit he said: ' It almost broke my jaw and took my teeth with it.'

ABA light heavyweight champion, Nicky Piper, the man who turned professional after taking the amateur title in 1989, boasts of an IQ of 153 and has been accepted as a member of the boffins club MENSA.

Ned Price, bare knuckle fighter of the mid 1880s could speak several languages including Chinese. He acted as interpreter in the criminal courts for some years, before becoming a lawyer himself.

During his pre fight instructions to 'Ageless' Archie Moore and Yolande Pompey who were about to do battle for Moore's heavyweight title in London, the referee asked if they were both conversant with the rules.

Moore, who had always been dubbed an old man, by the press, growled: 'Conversant – I wrote 'em!'

Irish flyweight Rinty Monaghan, who climbed to the top of the tree in 1948 by winning the world championship, loved to sing to the crowd after his bouts.

His singing voice was as good as his boxing and it got him a job touring with the services concert party ENSA, entertaining the troops.

American heavyweight Frank Moran, born in 1887 and fought around the turn of the century, started his working life as a dentist. But he soon learned that rearranging peoples teeth in the ring was more profitable.

Anyone who fought Terry Christie, the Irish/American, couldn't have asked for a better combination in an opponent. For having handed out a pasting, Terry could offer a medical service and advice on healing the cuts and bruises.

Because the Boston based battler was a qualified surgeon.

~ 🗡 ~

It could never be said that Ezzard Charles fiddled his fights – although he played the violin quite proficiently.

~ 🗡 ~

British light heavyweight champion of the early 1990s, boxings MENSA boffin, Nicky Piper, breeds rare canaries.

~ 🗡 ~

November 5, 1917 was a very busy day in the life of world champion Pete Herman. For, during that day he had two very important engagements.

In the morning he got married and in the evening he defended his world bantamweight title for a full twenty rounds against Frankie Burns.

It is not recorded what he did that night!

~ 🗡 ~

Sheffield based Karl Harris, Superbike rider for Honda, keeps himself fit for racing by cycling and wrestling. He is also an amateur boxer of note.

Sugar Ray Leonard is the only boxer to win world titles at five different weights: light heavy, super middle, middle, super welter and welterweight.

~ 🗡 ~

Bobby Czyz, a lightheavy and cruiser world title holder of the early 1990s, is a member of MENSA with an IQ of a little over 130.

He is the only boxing world champion in the Boffins Club.

~ 🗡 ~

Finchley based boxer, Roman Greenberg is fluent in four languages.

Flamboyant world champion Mike Tyson was so confident that he would defend his crown successfully and in record time, against James 'Buster' Douglas, in Tokyo on February 11, 1990 that he booked a flight home only three hours after the championship bout start time

History records that his confidence was a little on the optimistic side however and when he did return home it was without his title.

Former boxers, heavyweight tough guy Bruce Woodcock and middleweight Billy Carroll are brothers.

Italian Guido Ferracin won the European championship by outpointing Peter Kane at Manchester, in February 1948. Then, just to add insult to injury, he came back in July the same year and forced Kane to retire after five rounds.

There's nothing quite like hedging your bets by stating the obvious as examples of boxing commentators have shown in the past. BBC's Des Lynam enlightened television viewers with the startling revelation:

'Round one. Start of the fight, in fact.'

While at the other end of a different bout, former boxer turned commentator, Jim Watt summed up the situation thus:

'At the final bell, it was all over.'

Pearls of wisdom indeed. How would boxing fans understand the sport without them?

Jock McAvoy treated every one of his bouts as if it were for the world title, always giving his best and doing his utmost to win.

Tough guy McAvoy treated sparring sessions in the same manner, expecting no quarter and giving none. So it was no wonder that he found sparring partners difficult to come by.

Canadian Frankie Belanger had overcome the problem of getting his dressing gown off over gloved hands without a struggle as early as 1950. He had zip fasteners inserted in the ends of his sleeves.

There was never any wrestling and tugging in Frankies corner – just a quick zip and the gown was off.

Old time fighter Tom Sayers had the distinction of being buried in London's private burial ground, Higate Cemetery.

At his funeral his chief mourner was his bullmastiff, who led the cortège.

When Jimmy Wilde fought featherweight contender Joe Conn at Stamford Bridge in August 1918, there was a war on and the authorities insisted that the men should not box for a purse.

Wilde stopped his stone heavier opponent in twelve rounds but suffered a badly cut lip and a damaged eye in the process.

Two days later Mrs Wilde received two packets of diamonds from the promoters. The stones were valued at two thousand pounds.

Randall 'Tex' Cobb, the man who took the world champion Larry Holmes the full 15 rounds, in November 1982, was asked what he liked about boxing.

He replied: 'It sure beats working.'

Maxie Rosenbloom was in his dressing room, waiting to go on with Tiger Flowers, when two gangsters came in and told him that if he lost he would be well paid for his trouble.

When he refused they tapped bulges under the left shoulders and said: 'OK then but make sure you win. We'll bet on you – but make sure you get the decision or it will be too bad for you.'

Flowers was a very difficult man to beat and although Maxie tried everything he knew to put Flowers away, the close bout went the distance.

To his relief however, the referee called it a draw – and Maxie rushed over and kissed him.

Londons Royal Albert Hall first staged boxing in 1919 on, of all days, Boxing Day.

The bill included Ted 'Kid' Lewis and old-timer Matt Wells.

When former world heavyweight champion Sonny Liston died in 1970, his body was not removed for six days. Being a loner, no one was aware that he had died.

A mystery still surrounds the manner of his death.

The 1994 ABA championships had the novel distinction of having a Russian as a contestant.

Twenty five year old Mohammed Khamkhoer came to England to study and joined the Fitzroy Lodge amateur club, in November 1993.

His boxing standard was good enough to get him included in the ABA championships and his skill carried him right through to the finals where he just failed to clinch the super-heavyweight title.

Little Francis Ampofo beat the odds as well as his opponent when he dethroned Welshman Robbie Regan to take the British flyweight title at the National Sporting Centre, Cardiff, on September 4, 1991. Then he was told that he must do the whole thing over again.

The home crowd were so incensed at their local champion losing by a cut – sustained in the eleventh round, that they demanded a rematch and to save a possible riot, a rematch was agreed on the spot.

Tom Sharkey the famous Irish American heavyweight was not noted for his impeccable table manners.

One day he was shovelling food into his mouth with the aid of a long knife when someone asked him if he wasn't afraid that some well meaning friend might come up behind and slap him on the back at the very moment the point of the knife was furthest down his throat.

Tom replied: 'I've got nothing to worry about. All my friends are too well mannered to do a thing like that when I'm eating my dinner.'

When Brent Kosolofski won the vacant commonwealth title in a bout in Leeds, in 1993, little did he realise that very soon after he would be taking a dive.

For that is exactly what he did in his native Toronto soon after that bout – and from a third floor window no less.

The 29 year old had caused himself extensive injuries when the police found him in the road under the window where it appeared he had made his escape after an alleged burglary.

When Frankie Randall beat legendary Julio Cesar Chavez at Las Vegas in January 1994, he was 15 to 1 outsider.

For the rematch, in the same ring, in the following May, the odds had shortened considerably and Randall looked all set to prove that their first encounter was no fluke.

He was certainly holding his own against the Mexican whirlwind until an accidental clash of heads in the eighth round brought proceedings to a premature halt, with Chevez suffering a cut head.

The referee stopped the bout on the ringside doctors advice and Chavez regained his WBC light welterweight crown on a tot up of the judges scorecards.

Most boxers have good footwork but former British champion Les McAteer can surely claim the title of hot feet.

At a Boxing Federation gala at Southport, England, in the late 1980s Les, middleweight champion in 1969, slipped and fell into a boating lake. In his eagerness to dry off his shoes, Les put them in an oven but had overlooked the fact that they were of a man made material.

When he went back to collect his shoes all that was left were leather soles and a little puddle of melted plastic.

Billy Sim KO'd Bobby Frankham in the first round of their bout at Wembley in December 1987. Previously unbeaten Frankham was so upset he jumped up and punched the referee.

Fights also started in sections of the crowd and Frankham was subsequently banned for life.

Former ABA middleweight champion Johnny Prices hopes were short lived as he stepped through the ropes at Alexandra Pavilion on April 25 1984 to face former WBA world champ Ayub Kalule. Because the first punch he received knocked him back through the ropes and signalled the end of the contest.

Ingemar Johansson took the heavyweight championship of the world from Floyd Patterson in three rounds, in New York on June 26, 1959. That third round win included seven knockdowns, which proves that the Swede was no slouch.

But it was a different story in the 1952 Olympic Games in Helsinki. Johansson as an amateur, fought his way to the heavyweight final but then had the indignity of being disqualified for 'not trying'.

The last twenty round contest to be staged at The Ring, Blackfriars, took place on a Sunday afternoon. The date was February 28, 1929 and Londoner Johnny Curley fought Welshman Alby Kestrell the full distance, for a draw.

The unluckiest man of all time must be Richie Kates. Richie was knocked out in the very last second of a fifteen round world title bout against Victor Golindez on May 22, 1976.

Willie Meehan started out as a flyweight but a stretch in the US Navy, where he must have liked navy food, saw him balloon to an overweight heavyweight.

Despite the accurate, if unwanted, title of 'Fat Willie' Meehan was no easy ride as his epic battles with Jack Dempsey, at the end of World War One shows.

Of their three clashes Meehan took the decision in their last bout, which was no easy task and one that so-called better men had failed to do.

Tall, Taller, Tallest

But for a foul Buddy Baer would have had the distinction of being the tallest world champion. May 23, 1941 in Washington, six feet six and a half inches tall Buddy knocked champion Joe Louis out of the ring and could have possibly taken the world title a couple of rounds later.

However, at the end of the sixth round Louis landed a blow after the bell and Baer played up the foul and refused to start the seventh round – thereby losing his chance of getting into the record books.

Primo Carnera, standing at six feet five and three quarter inches, is usually talked about as the tallest world champion, but Jess Willard was six feet six and a quarter inches which makes him half an inch taller and gives him the honours as the tallest ever world champion.

However, Carnera had the edge on the scales. The 'Ambling Alp' had a fifteen pounds advantage over the 'Kansas Cowboy' weighing in at 19 stones 1 pound against Willards 18 stones.

James J Willard may have been the tallest world champion but at six feet six and a quarter inches he was nowhere near the tallest ever professional boxer.

There have been several boxers over the years that have stood 6 feet 6 inches, including British boxer Jack Pettifer who fought Jack Patterson in the 1930s, and American Ernie Tyrell, who unsuccessfully challenged Ali for world honours, was also 6 feet 6 inches. American Charles Freeman, star of the 1840s towered above them at 6 feet 10 inches but South African Ewart Potgieter dwarfed them all at a lofty 7 feet 2 inches.

The *'shortest'* world champion was Thailand's light-flyweight Netroni Vorasingh, who scaled the heights at 4 feet eleven inches.

When Floyd Patterson lost his heavyweight title to Ingemar Johansson, on June 26, 1959 in New York, with the big Swede stopping the native New Yorker in the third round, Floyd seemed to receive more support in defeat than the new champ did in victory.

Even the Swedes in the audience appeared to applaud Patterson more than their own countryman despite the fact that he had just won the heavyweight world championship.

Patterson was so impressed with this show of affection that he went to live in Sweden after the bout. He stayed there for over a year.

The fastest end to a bout ever must surely be Eddie Vann's removal of George Stern. This took place on November 15, 1949 at Harringay Arena and after referee Pat Fox had finished counting out Stern, only twelve seconds had elapsed.

The shortest British title fight on record was held at Nottingham on November 20, 1961, when lightweight Dave Charnley disposed of Dave Hughes in 40 seconds.

A decade earlier, on August 28 1951, Tommy McGovern finished his bout and took the honours against Billy Thompson in 55 seconds, in London.

Jersey Joe Walcott was the oldest boxer to win the heavyweight world champion. He was only a couple of weeks short of being thirty seven year and six months old when he took the title from Ezzard Charles on July 18, 1951, via a seventh round KO, in Pittsburg – and he was a year older when he repelled a challenge from Charles in a return a year later, in Philadelphia, on June 5, 1952.

After his world championship bout with American John C Heenan, at Farnborough, England, on April 17, 1860, the fans of Tom Sayers had a collection that amounted to £2,000. This they presented to him on condition that he never fought again.

True to his word Tom Sayers never fought again.

When Don Jordan won the world welterweight championship on December 5, 1958 he became a very happy – and wealthy – man.

Unlike his situation a couple of years earlier when, mixing with the criminal element in Mexico, he had to borrow 300 dollars to get himself back home to Los Angeles.

Talk about being kicked in the face.

Welshman Andy Morgan won the kick boxing world championship, only to find that his professional boxing license had been withdrawn.

There ain't no justice.

Cork, Ireland erected a commerative plaque to their world champion local boy, Jack McAuliffe.

McAuliffe, world lightweight champion throughout the 1880s, died in New York more than 50 years prior to the Irish getting around to erecting their tribute to the little man.

Once when Max Baer was fighting Joe Louis he had Jack Dempsey in his corner for moral support.

Baer spent a very apprehensive first round and when he got back to his corner, Dempsey told him: 'You're doing fine pal. Just keep making him miss.'

Louis gave Baer an even harder time in the next round but still Dempsey insisted: 'That's the idea pal. Move around and he won't hit you all evening.' Max gave him a quizzical look.

When he came back to his corner at the end of the third round, Baer's left eye was cut, his nose swollen and his lips were bleeding.

So when Dempsey, trying to cheer up his pal, said: 'He hasn't laid a glove on you yet, Maxie.' Baer replied: 'Do me a favour will you Jack. Keep your eye on the referee during the next round, because if it isn't Louis then someone is sure knocking the hell out of me.'

It was all over in the next round with the referee stopping it to save Maxie further punishment.

Don McCorkindale was getting the better of Larry Gains in their 1952 Empire heavyweight title fight when there was a great commotion outside the ropes, in Gains corner. Don automatically eased up and the bell came to Larrys rescue.

Ted Broadribb, McCorkindales cornerman thought his man had won as he reached his corner and shouted: 'You've won, Gains is going to retire.'

But it was nothing of the sort.

Gains was looking over the ropes to a tragic scene by the ringside. His trainer, Jack Goodwin, overcome by excitement, had died from a heart attack.

The contest continued without the spectators aware of the death in their midst and Gains won narrowly on points.

In March 1988 welterweights Mike Russell and Mark Purcell clashed in the centre of the ring at Bournemouth – and it was a real clash.

Their heads met with such force that Russell slumped to the floor with concussion and the bout went no further.

Twenty-six year old Michael Moorer upset the odds when he beat heavyweight world champion Evander Holyfield in Las Vegas on April 22, 1994, to become WBA and IBF champion.

He also beat the odds by becoming the first southpaw to win the world heavyweight title.

Heavyweight world champion Tommy Burns defended his title eleven times in succession, the last seven times were outside of America.

Having taken the title from Marvin Hart in California he then defended four more times in California. Then, moving abroad he defended against:

Gunner Moir	December 2, 1907	NSC London
Jack Palmer	February 10, 1908	Wonderland London
Jem Roach	March 17, 1908	Dublin
Jewey Smith	April 18, 1908	Paris
Bill Squires	June 13, 1908	Paris
Bill Squires	August 24, 1908	Sydney Australia
Bill Lang	September 2, 1908	Melbourne Australia

He finally lost his crown to Jack Johnson in Sydney Australia on (of all days) Boxing Day 1908.

Southern promoter Tony Doodney has a superb collection of boxing prints, possibly the largest privately owned collection anywhere. He is reluctant to have them valued because, he said: 'the figure would probably frighten the life out of me – but I do know that the frames are worth in excess of £10,000.'

Sonny Liston, world heavyweight champion 1962 – 1964, had the largest hands of any world champion since boxing gloves were made compulsory.

His enormous clenched fist measured fifteen inches and was so big that gloves had to be specially made for him because he could not get his hands into the regulation standard gloves.

Former leading snooker player, Eddie Charlton has played most sports at competitive level.

Apart from his exploits on the green baize, Aussie Eddie was a member of the crew that won the Australian Senior Surfboat championships in 1950. He also had the distinction of having carried the Olympic Torch for one mile into Swansea, New South Wales, prior to the 1956 Melbourne Olympic Games.

Edie was also a competent boxer and once boxed four rounds against Commonwealth middleweight champion, Dave Sands.

Joseph Berardinelli was the real name of Joey Maxim, the man who deprived Freddie Mills of the world lightheavyweight championship in London, on January 24, 1950.

Harry Greb, world middleweight champion 1923 – 1926, died in hospital under anaesthetic whilst having his nose repaired.

The fight of the long count, when Jack Dempsey put Gene Tunney down for what transpired to be a fourteen second count at Soldiers Field, Chicago, on September 22, 1927, has been well chronicled over the years.

Suffice it to record that Dempsey put Tunney down in the seventh round of the Tex Rickard promotion and referee Dave Barry would not start the count until Dempsey went to the farthest neutral corner, as had been previously agreed.

By the time Dempsey had sorted himself out and got to the correct place about five seconds had elapsed before the count could start. Tunney finally rose when the count reached nine, thereby giving himself those extra valuable seconds.

It is also recorded that almost 105,000 fans watched the bout that was the first two and a half million dollar gate – then an all time record.

It is said that Tunney, the eventual winner, received 990,445 dollars for his share of the gate and he gave promoter Rickard a cheque for the balance so that he could be paid with a million dollar cheque which – after cashing it of course, he had framed.

After being stopped inside a round, Jeff Thompson, a 1991 light heavyweight challenger, cracked: 'He did to me what I thought I was going to do to him.'

Change of Career

Henry Armstrong, the first man to hold three world titles at the same time, started his professional career the dishonest way – by taking dives on orders from his manager. Later he must have decided that honesty was the best policy because he threw off his old way of life, changed his name to Armstrong and went on to record treble world honours in double quick time.

The honesty route must have suited Henry because after his retirement from the ring he became a parson.

~ 🕴 ~

Henry Hall, British welterweight champion 1948-49, was also a qualified football referee.

~ 🕴 ~

Rick Ferrell, who was honoured in Baseballs Hall of Fame in 1984, helped to pay his way through college way back in the 1920s by boxing. He fought as a lightweight and notched up 17 straight wins before taking up baseball and achieving national honours.

~ 🕴 ~

Londoner Clay O'Shea may not have changed careers although he has several to chose from.

The light middleweight, who turned pro in 1990, is a committed Christian. He said: 'God gave me a talent, so I shall use it.'

This quiet unassuming man is a talented golfer; plays cricket and played in a pop group.

He became vegetarian around the same time that he turned pro and, to top it all, stopped his first professional opponent in just 25 seconds.

~ 🕴 ~

Clown princes of the ring, the two Maxs, Baer and Rosenbloom, carried on their clowning after retiring from the ring.

They entertained around the nightclubs as a double act.

~ 🕴 ~

After being dethroned by Irelands Barry McGuigan at Queens Park Rangers football ground, in London on June 8, 1985, Panamaian Eusebio Pedrosa turned to a different kind of fighting, but still ended up on the losing end.

He became one of Colonel Noreigas personal bodyguards, just prior to the colonel being ousted in the invasion by American troops in 1989.

Johnny Nuttall, the Indian born middleweight, was also a first class cricketer and good enough to play for India. He also played hockey at International level.

Paul Nihill started his boxing career with an amateur club in his hometown of Croydon but quickly learned that he much preferred pounding pavements with his feet, to having opponents pounding his face with their fists.

He liked the roadwork part of his training so much that after a while he changed sports to accommodate his new found passion.

He entered race walk competitions, eventually becoming good enough to win selection for the England squad where he went on to win the Silver Medal in the 1964 Olympic Games 50 kilometre walk, held in Tokyo.

Later Paul went into the record books as the first British male athlete to compete in four consecutive Olympic Games. He was awarded an MBE for his services to sport.

Paolino Uzcudun, the Spanish heavyweight, became chief of police in Valencia, after his retirement from the ring.

American lightweight, Ben Caulfield was a professor of biblical studies.

~ 🕴 ~

It is not recorded how much Gene Tunney made from boxing. But what is known is that when he retired from the ring he was a very wealthy man.

He married an heiress who was worth TEN MILLION!

~ 🕴 ~

Bombadier Billy Wells was as handy on the track as he was in the ring. As well as his success as a boxer he was also a very competent runner.

When James J Willard fought Frank Moran on the Tex Rickard promotion in the old Madison Square Garden, New York on March 25, 1916, the bout went the full distance. Newspapers declared Willard the distance winner but, at that time, decision bouts were against the law in New York – hence the no decision verdict.

Although most people remember Rinty Monaghan usually gave his fans a song after his bouts, the original singing boxer was Fred Dyer.

Charlie Jordan, Kingston featherweight of note in the 1930s, was one of the first boxers in England to own a foul protection belt.

These belts, worn under the shorts and in common use these days were introduced in the USA in the early 1930s. Charlie had friends in America and they sent him one and he soon made good use of it in his following bouts.

He had lost a decision to Chathams featherweight and Silver Belt holder, Bert 'Kid' Freeman and was anxious to avenge himself. Next time the pair met, the good-humoured banter began.

'I'll get you tonight,' said Charlie

'You'll have to steam Charlie,' was the instant reply.

All went well for a couple of rounds then, in the third round 'Kid' threw a punch, which Charlie saw coming. Somehow he managed to hoist himself up causing the blow to land low.

'Kid' remembered: 'Charlie immediately threw himself on the canvas in an agony pantomime worthy of an Oscar and, naturally, I was disqualified. Later Charlie came into my dressing room and, with a big grin said he had told me he would get me. Then he showed me his foul proof belt and I could have hit it with a hammer and not hurt him.'

Bert 'Kid' Freeman was a little upset at having his record spoilt because that was the only disqualification ever registered against him. But, like the true sportsman that he was, he says: ' I've no regrets really. It was all part of the game; they were real pros.'

Glen McCrory did everything possible to ensure he was at peak fitness before his attempt to become British and European heavyweight champion. This included 'signing-up' for a months physical training with the army at their Catterrick camp in Yorkshire, England.

Unfortunately Lennox Lewis could not be out manoeuvred on the night and all of McCrorys square bashing torture proved to be in vain.

A Harry Lavene promotion made boxing history in 1946 when, in Brighton, England, on June 25th the ring collapsed.

The bout in progress at the time was a heavyweight clash between Reg Andrews and Ernie Woodman when, in the second round, the ring gave way completely with the remainder of that bout and the rest of the programme having to be cancelled.

A local newspaper reported the incident with a cartoon drawing of Ernie shaping up to a pair of legs that were sticking out of the canvas. Above it was the caption ': Believe it or not – it really happened.'

Mario D'Agata, Italian bantamweight world champ in the mid 1950s, is deaf and dumb.

Featherweight Robert Dickies father is a Scot but Robert lived in Wales and spoke Welsh.

Dan Sherry, the man who lost his chance of becoming world champion after being on the receiving end of the much publicised Eubank head-butt in Brighton, continued his run of bad luck on his next trip to England a year later.

Canadian Sherry stepped off his flight at Heathrow Airport and lost his hand luggage containing all his money.

Whilst training for the forthcoming season on the West Country boxing booths, boxer turned author Harry Legge tripped and injured the ligaments in his chest.

Rather than take the prescribed rest and wait for the injury to heal, Harry hit upon a plan to make an armoured breastplate. This he fashioned from a saucepan lid and, after a few adjustments with a hammer he taped the moulded lid to his chest and hid it under a T-shirt, so that he could continue boxing.

All went well for several bouts until the tape lost its adhesiveness and the home made breastplate slipped from his chest and lodged in his foul proof belt.

At the end of that particular bout the saucepan lid breastplate took on a mind of its own and fell out of the leg of Harry's shorts.

Harry recalled: 'I quickly picked it up and hid it under my dressing gown and, as it was a nobbins bout, I suggested that my opponent and I got into collecting the nobbins as quickly as possible before the audience started drifting away. That bit of quick thinking and the thought of extra money to be collected forestalled any awkward questions about my unofficial armour,'

Canadian Solly Cantor made his first trip to England in 1948 and was met off the boat train by a sister that he had not seen before.

Years later their positions were reversed, Solly settled in England and his sister, Hilda, moved to the other side of the Atlantic.

After his boxing days were over Solly Cantor had his nose repaired with a bit of bone taken from his backside.

Years after that successful operation he was still cracking the same old joke. 'Every time I get tired, my nose wants to sit down.'

Former world middleweight champion, tough guy Nigel Benn was quoted as saying: 'God put Nigel Benn on this earth to kick butt and kick butt good!'

Norman Wisdom, knockabout star of stage and screen, was also a very good boxer in his youth. He well remembers his first fight when he learned the 'price' of fame in the ring.

He remembers: 'As a 14 year old cabin boy I was on a ship out of Cardiff and headed for Beunos Aires in the Argentine. During the voyage the crew taught me more-or-less how to box which, at the time, I thought was very kind of them.

When we arrived they took me off to a boxing booth and entered me to fight one of the booth's professionals. It was for a three rounder, and in those days any challenger who stood up to the booth fighter for one round was paid about a pound, for two rounds about two pounds and for staying the distance the prize was a fiver.

I'm sure that my opponent was a couple of stones heavier than me but never-the-less I gave it my best, with the crew cheering me on. Although I was smashed to the ground several times and smothered with blood from the terrible beating that I was taking, I was still able to clamber to my feet at the end of the third round before the referee had counted to ten.

My shipmates cheered and shouted as I headed away to have a bath and get dressed but, when I came out to be greeted by my pals I found alas, that they has collected my winnings and disappeared to the nearest pub, and as I was unable to find them I had to return to the ship on my own.

Never-the-less when they ruffled my hair in a congratulatory fashion the next morning I didn't care abut the money at all – somehow I felt that I had become a man.'

Jack Broughton was acknowledged as the Father of Boxing, partly through laying down the early rules governing the sport, many of which constitute the basis of the present day rules.

Broughton was one of the earliest boxing champions and he became champion of England soon after James Figg had put the sport onto a recognised foundation, in the early 1700s.

He became tutor to the Duke of Cumberland, who later became King George the Third. This 'chalk and cheese' pairing formed a lifelong friendship and, after his retirement from the ring, Broughton was employed in the Kings service.

Jack Broughton was further honoured by being buried in Westminster Abbey.

Philipino 'Flash' Elorde, who held the world junior lightweight championship for most of the 1960s, is reputed to have taken part in a title bout every year of his professional boxing career.

When Leon Spinks took the world heavyweight title from Muhammad Ali, on February 15, 1978, he had engaged in only seven professional bouts.

Whip Round – a term in everyday use these days probably originated from bare knuckle fighting times.

In those days a ring usually consisted of a single strand of rope marking out a square in a field or barn. To keep spectators away from the contestants another ring would be erected around the outside, about three to four feet away. In this outer ring, what we these days would refer to as bouncers patrolled with whips to protect the contestants and officials.

After a particularly good fight these bouncers would pass the hat round for an early version of nobbins.

These people were known as whips for obvious reasons and, with a cap in one hand and a whip in the other, they would have a 'whip round'.

Bruce Wells, the man who ruled the amateur section of the sport throughout the 1950s, took part in 388 contests and chalked up victories in all but three of them.

He also took part in 100 international bouts and was victorious in all but one!

WA and WS Pullum

WA (Bill) Pullum was a top class amateur weightlifter before World War One. At that time there was no one in the world that could have prevented him from taking top honours and he was only denied an Olympic Gold Medal because the Olympic Games were not held.

However, as he was unable to compete in the Olympics, he did the next best thing. He became team coach for the British Olympic weightlifting team for the 1948 Olympic Games that were held in London. His team took third place.

Almost all the British weightlifting champions were trained by 'Bill' Pullum right up until his death in 1960 at the age of 74.

Retired weightlifting champion of the world WA (Bill) Pullum took up boxing promotions at Rochester Casino in the late 1930s and, in one of his early shows, had managed to engage the services of the very popular 'Seaman' Tommy Watson, to top the bill over 15 rounds.

Watson, who was to go on to the British featherweight title and later to fight for world honours, had worked a good deal for himself that meant a guaranteed wage plus a percentage of the gate receipts. As expected Watson stopped his opponent early and was soon round to the promoters office to collect his money and, being a dour north countryman with an eye on business at all times, he had checked the gate takings and had already worked out his share.

Promoter Pullum said; 'Sorry Tommy but our figures don't agree with yours.'

An aggressive 'Seaman' replied: 'These are my figures and that's the amount that I want. I'm not leaving this office until I get it.'

With a grin on his face, promoter Pullum replied: 'OK, if you insist but I make it five pounds more than you demand.'

Watson didn't know where to put his face but northern business sense conquered his embarrassment and he accepted the extra money before leaving.

WS Pullum (Young Billy), the son of champion weightlifter WA Pullum was promoting in partnership at Oxford Town Hall in 1936 when his show was struck with a promoters nightmare – all the bouts finished quickly and the entire card finished early .

Top of the bill Johnny Rust of South Africa KO'd Ivor Pickens, the welter-weight champion of Wales in the first round and Corporal George Robey of Oxford had to retire early after almost losing an eyelid in another main contest. Most of the supporting bouts finished ahead of the scheduled time.

This left 'Young Billy' to face an unhappy section of the crowd, so he took the unprecedented step of jumping into the ring and issuing a challenge to have someone from the audience box him.

Billy said: 'When I got them quietened down, I asked if they had been happy with the previous shows; they answered that they had.

'But you didn't like this one,' I asked. 'No' was the loud reply.

I pointed out that the same matchmaker (me) put together all programmes. I told them I had billed Johnny Rust as South African KO King – and he had proved it. I also told them that no genuine sportsman would expect a boxer to continue with a badly cut eye. However, I conceded that it was customary to put on an extra bout when the fights finished early, but that we had no spare boxers.

But I told them there was a solution: I put myself up as one contestant for an extra bout and appealed for anyone from the audience to be my opponent. I shouted come on, don't be shy, there's a whole bunch of boxing experts up there in the gallery where all the uproar has been coming from.

No one came forward. The mass of the audience applauded me and all went away peacefully.

WS 'Young Billy' Pullum was promoting at East Ham Baths in the 1930s, when for one of his forthcoming attractions he devised a 'Royal Navy versus The Rest' show.

Royal Navy middleweight champion 'Seaman' Joe Wakeling was asked to help with the navy team but at the end of the day they were still one boxer short.

'Young Billy' said: 'I just billed an imaginary sailor, hoping someone would turn up at the last minute. I billed my imaginary sailor as 'Seaman' Drake but I forgot to tell Joe Wakeling.

Then on the night of the show Wakeling arrived with the navy boxers and supporters but he told me he had searched all over the ships in Chatham Dockyard but couldn't find the elusive 'Seaman' Drake anywhere.

I told him that I thought he might have trouble as 'Seaman' Drake had been dead for about 300 years.'

Wakeling didn't find 'Young Billys' sense of humour very funny and after that night he would always check the forthcoming bills .... 'just to see if that bloody Pullum had slipped in a 'Seaman' Nelson into my team.'

Seaman
Joe Wakelin

THE
Rochester Casino.

KENT'S MOST
COMMODIOUS
Boxing Hall.

Run every Monday for Boxing
by

W. A. PULLUM,

**The name that enjoys the complete confidence
of the Sporting Public whenever and
wherever it appears.**

PROGRAMME

FOR

MONDAY EVENING

MARCH 23rd, 1931.

Price—ONE PENNY.

Casino

Rochester MP Mr Forde Ridley, officially opened the Casino in Rochester, Kent, on May 23, 1910, and very soon 'boxing and Casino' became synonymous with boxers from all over the country and even farther afield appearing on the bill.

From the 1920s until the late 1940s boxing was the main attraction and complimented other entertainments such as dancing and roller-skating.

Mrs Bella Burge of The Ring fame also promoted at the Casino. Bella was one of two lady promoters that staged boxing there. The other lady promoter was Mrs Emma Jacobs.

Mrs Emma Jacobs introduced a young Billy Webb to her patrons at the Casino and Billy repaid her kindness by quickly stamping his authority on the place.

In a five-year career 1930 to 1934, with one bout in 1935, Billy appeared at the Casino an incredible 64 times. That colossal achievement earned him the title 'King of the Casino' – a name that stuck with him right up until his death some sixty odd years later.

Mrs Emma Jacobs gave Billy Webb his break on her penultimate show and her faith in him was justified when he scored the only stoppage on that night's bill. A couple of weeks later Billy was invited back on to new promoter Mac`s opening show.

Four Swinbourne brothers fought on the same bill at Rochester Casino; this was February 3, 1930. It was not a particularly auspicious occasion and certainly not one for the family album, as they went into the record books with three points losses and one draw on that historic night.

Later five Buxton brothers appeared on the same bill at a show but even that was bettered when six Fielding brothers were on the same bill in Wrexham.

'King of the Casino' Billy didn't just lay back on his laurels and wait for his new-found title to grow around him. He was happy to meet almost anyone anywhere.

In the Casino ring in front of his home fans he met Goff Williams, Tommy Gardner (twice), Billy Goble (twice) and Dave Penfield – all Kent champions.

A couple of days before Christmas 1930 the Casino bill had to be improvised when due to a very heavy fog the show had to be made up from boxers that were already in the venue; some who had only come as spectators. In those days 'off-duty' boxers would turn up with their kit stuffed in their pockets, or in a small bag, hoping for last minute substitute job. That night their luck was in.

Billy, a featherweight, was matched against bantamweight champion of Kent, Jimmy Turner. Turner just got the nod over six hotly contested rounds.

'Kid' Freeman, himself a 27 time veteran of the Casino, recalled the time when a cruiser was found to have a sailmaker's leather palm on his hand, inside the glove.

When challenged he protested: 'I only wear that to protect my thumb.'

December 16, 1929 was a turning point in the life of Eddie Philips. Eddie a coach driver, who had brought a coach load of fans to see the show, was talked into taking a last minute substitute job. He liked the experience so much that he took it up as a career and went on to become British light-heavyweight champion.

A few years later as an established boxer, Eddie was at a London show that featured several Casino regulars. After the show he offered the Kent boys a ride home in his van.

'Kid' Freeman recalled: 'We didn't know who he was but a ride home instead of waiting for the 4.30 am train was too good an opportunity to miss and we gladly accepted. On the way home we learned that he was Eddie Philips and also that he had to go straight back to start work at 5.30 am at his job in Covent Garden.

Throughout his boxing career 'King of the Casino' Billy Webb was only ever knocked out once. That was when he was laid low in 20 seconds, on December 1 1930, by Bow battler, Johnny Kilbane.

Even at that reversal, inveterate comic Billy could make a joke of it all.

'I was the highest paid boxer on that night's show,' he cracked. 'After all, how many people get paid for less than half a minutes work?'

November 18, 1929 local boy Tug Willson lost to Ireland's Mick McCullough at the Casino but had the consolation of hearing MC Joe Wilson give a round by round summary of the Primo Carnera v Young Stribling bout, relayed from the Albert Hall.

Casino – Rochester, Kent

74

Every one remembers the historic occasion when British champion Henry Cooper decked world champion Cassius Clay, in their heavyweight clash at Wembley, on May 21, 1966.

It was toward the end of the fifth round and everyone remembers that the bell probably saved Clay.

Everyone also knows that Clay's corner got their man a lot of extra time by saying his glove was split and asking for a replacement pair.

But what the vast majority of people don't know is that those split gloves became sought after by collectors – and at one stage after that historic bout, there were at least a dozen pairs of split gloves in circulation, all claiming to be that original pair.

The original Madison Square Garden was situated at Madison Avenue and 27 Street up until 1924. It was then demolished and a new one built on the same site, in 1925.

The current Madison Square garden was built on a new site, incorporating Penn Station on 7th Avenue, in 1968.

October 4, 1940 is a date that two well known boxers have cause to remember – but for completely different reasons,

On the same bill in New York on that significant night Sugar Ray Robinson won his professional debut and Henry Armstrong lost his world title on his 21st defence.

Twenty years after that controversial split gloves bout between Cassius Clay, who later became Muhammad Ali, and Henry Cooper, Clay's trainer Angelo Dundee finally told the truth about what really happened during that fourth round interval, that night at Wembley.

In his book 'I only talk winning' published in September 1983, Dundee tells all.

He says: 'I saw a small slit along the seam of the boxing glove. I stuck my finger in the slit to help it along. I yelled for referee Tommy Little to examine the glove. I yelled at everybody; I wanted a new pair of gloves.

I don't know how many minutes I gained.....I admit it was gamesmanship.'

Gentleman Jim Corbett sparred an exhibition with the almost invincible John L Sullivan and, after the bout was over history books record that Corbett said: 'I can beat him, he's a sucker for a feint.'

Whether he actually said that is not known for sure but what is for sure is that he did beat Sullivan, in September 1892, by a knockout in the 21st round.

Archie Sexton, the first man to box on television with Laurie Raiteri, way back in 1933, was fighting at The Ring, Blackfriars in the late 1930s and he was in all kinds of trouble.

At the end of the round he told his manager, Johnny Sharpe, that he wanted to retire from the bout but manager Sharpe convinced him to have one more round, saying: 'I know it hurts Archie. I feel it as much as you do.'

Just at precise moment there was one of those uncanny silences and Archie could be heard all over the hall saying in a very loud voice: 'I wish you did, you bastard.'

Battersea Bulldog, Ernie Woodman, reveals that his biggest battle was not in the ring at all. One of his early skirmishes was in the street, and that encounter he remembered above all his other memorable bouts because he went down to a lot of extra weight.

Although a heavyweight himself, many years after Ernie could see the funny side of the whole affair and how he just couldn't handle his opponents superior power.

His opponent on that auspicious occasion was a London tram. The tram won and Ernie lost two toes and part of his foot. But despite such crippling bad luck Ernie still went on to a successful boxing career and was also a PTI with the army in World War II.

Even as a lad Ernie had that fighting spirit and, to compensate for his injured foot, he devised a way of getting about on one roller skate, propelling himself along with his other foot.

However, his dad had something to say about that, because it was playing havoc with shoe repair bills. 'From now on it's two skates or nothing.' He ordered.

So young Ernie donned both skates and taught himself to skate properly. He became so proficient that after a while he was able to perform in public, soon attaining expert status.

When Jack Dempsey won the world heavyweight title from James J Willard, Dempseys manager bet their purse money on Dempsey to win in the first round.

Dempsey thought he had won in the first and left the ring. However, he had to be called back to continue for a further two rounds.

Although he won conclusively Dempsey got nothing from the fight – because the bet stipulated a first round win.

Heavyweight ace of the 1990s Gary Masons boxing career almost came to an end before it had even started.

He recalls: 'When I first started my early training with an amateur club my regular sparring partner beat me up all the time and I was beginning to have doubts about whether I was in the right line of business. The trainers convinced me to keep at it and I agreed to enter my first official bout.

You can imagine how frightened I was when, in front of an audience, my opponent turned out to be that same sparring partner.

Somehow I managed to conquer my fear and for the first time ever, I beat him. That made me feel pretty good and I went on to win ten bouts before discharging my amateur vest.'

When he first turned pro, Gary Mason lived alone except for a boxer dog named Champ.

Old bare knuckle fighter of the early 1800s, Tom Hickman had his own favourite punch that he named 'The Whisker Punch' thereby starting a trend.

Here are a few more named punches, with their equally famous operator:

Cork Screw	'Kid' McCoy
Scissors	Battling Nelson
Solar Plexus	Bob Fitzsimmons
Mary Ann	Frank Moran
Suzy Q	Rocky Marciano
Lowestoft Loop	Jim Lawlor
Thors Hammer	Ingemar Johansson

November 5, 1946 Freddie Mills had a private firework display all to himself, when he lost in six rounds to giant American Joe Baski, at Harringay.

Mills, who had never been afraid of a fight and had mixed it with some of the best, said after the 'Baski Blitz' that he had never been hit so hard before.

He told reporters: 'I could virtually feel his knuckles through his gloves.'

Freddie Welsh was such a good boxer that respective lightweight champions would not accept a challenge from him. So desperate was he to get a crack at the world title that he offered champion Willie Richie a purse that Richie just could not refuse.

What Richie didn't know was that he received all the money and Freddie fought for nothing just to get his chance at the title, which he won by the narrowest of margins, in London on July 7, 1914.

Skint

Jack Donn, who went on to a successful career that lasted for fifteen years and included several twenty rounders, remembers well his first paid bout.

He was standing outside a London railway station, completely broke, when a man approached him to enquire if he would like to earn a bob or two by undertaking a four rounder at Stephney Social Club. Like most people, Jack was fond of eating on a regular basis so he agreed although he had never boxed before.

He was paid seven shillings and sixpence for the fight and he must have put up a good show because a spectator was so impressed with his fighting qualities that he slipped a ten shilling note into Jacks pocket.

The week following his first bout, the Donn family lived better than usual with several meat puddings to eat and even a plum duff for afters.

These, they tell us, were the good old days.

When Jack Dempsey fought Tom Gibbons in Shelby, Montana, on July 4, 1923, the well known 'Doc' Kearns was his manager.

Kearns, who was a very shrewd businessman, insisted upon full payment before he would allow his boxer to enter the ring. As it turned out that was a very wise move because the town was on the verge of bankruptcy and the banks had no cash.

Kearns collected Dempsey's money but for Gibbons, who still on his feet at the end of fifteen rounds, there was no money left.

At the Velodrome D'Hiver, Paris on June 6, 1914, two world famous boxers squared off for their title bout.

Jack Johnson and Frank Moran were the combatants and the 'third man' was the equally well known 'Orchid Man' Georges Carpentier.

Johnson won the day but there were no real winners because the authorities impounded all the money.

Before the case could be brought before the courts, World War One started and everything was put on hold.

Right up until their deaths, many years later, neither boxer received that money.

Although strictly an amateur, Bruce Wells had his moments with the professionals.

In 1978 he boxed a charity exhibition with the legendary Muhammad Ali. Former world champ Terry Downes was the referee.

A quarter of a century earlier, in an International match against Poland, hard-up Bruce shared a pair of boxing shorts with yet-to-be British Champion Henry Cooper.

Fred Atkins ABA judge and one-time Merchant Navy's Orient Line light heavyweight champion , was with his ship in Sydney, Australia and, being a keen boxer, he found his way to the Banksdown gymnasium. Training in the gym was a young Aborigine light heavyweight chap who didn't appear to have any decent boxing kit.

Fred recalled: 'I let this fellow borrow my trunks and dressing gown but, as the ship I was on had to leave soon after I didn't have time to get my gear back so I had to leave it there.

A few years later I was at home watching a professional show from London, on television when this same chap appeared in the ring – still wearing my trunks and dressing gown.'

Joshua Kisini, amateur welterweight boxer from the Solomon Islands, turned up at the Commonwealth Games in Auckland, New Zealand in 1989, with no money and no gloves.

He told baffled officials that he had hitchhiked all the way to be at the Games. He had only just arrived in time to take part because his scheduled bout was the next day.

His first bout however, turned out to be his one and only. He was KOd in the third round.

He was so pleased to have made it in time to take part that he said he was delighted with his performance.

~ 🏏 ~

On January 11, 1945 Jersey Joe Walcott made a come back in his hometown of Camden, New Jersey, by delivering a second round knockout to Jackie Saunders. The purse for that fight was a bit odd in that Joe had been paid in advance – and his fee was a ton of coal.

After spending 14 years in the business and nothing to show for it, Joe was finished with boxing. He was down on his luck and living with his family in the poorer end of town, when a local promoter found him and offered him a bout.

Jersey Joe, now 30 years of age, was disillusioned and wanted nothing further to do with the game but he eventually agreed to give it another go, on the grounds that he was broke and had nothing to lose.

What a wise move that turned out to be because two years later, almost to the day, he was fighting Joe Louis for the world heavyweight title.

Having spent so long in the shadows as an also-ran, it was no wonder that he was disillusioned. But under the guidance of a new manager, things happened quickly.

Jersey Joe fought his way into the spotlight and became heavyweight champion of the world on July 18, 1951 by stopping Ezzard Charles in seven rounds, in Pittsburgh. He reigned supreme then for a little over a year until Rocky Marciano deposed him in the thirteenth round, on September 23, 1952, in Philadelphia.

All in all Joe fought for world honours on eight occasions – and it all came about because he needed some coal to keep his family warm.

Rocky Marciano retired from boxing at the very pinnacle of his career, in 1956. He was 32 years old, he'd had 49 wins and no defeats and he retired as current heavyweight world champion – having made more than £3 million dollars.

It is alleged that he made millions more from personal appearances after he had retired, charging from £1,000 to £7,500 a time.

But his Midas Touch didn't extend to his business ventures. He had pulled out of several businesses just prior to his death in a plane crash in 1969, including an hotel in New York, a restaurant in Maryland, a bowling alley in Florida and a potato farm 'mostly because they had lost so much money.'

James J Braddock started his boxing career as a welterweight and rose through the ranks – and weights – to become world heavyweight champion in 1935. He started boxing in 1926 and boxed for several years with little success, then retired broke.

Braddock made a return to the ring in 1934 and, with only three bouts into his come-back, beat Max Baer for the world title.

World champion Larry Holmes defended his crown eight times as an undefeated champion, where his challenger (up to that time) was also undefeated. The unsuccessful challengers were:

LeRoy Jones	March 31, 1980	24 wins and 1 draw
Renaldo Snipes	November 6, 1981	22 wins
Gerry Cooney	June 11, 1982	25 wins
Tim Witherspoon	May 20, 1983	15 wins
Scott Frank	September 10, 1983	20 wins and 1 draw
Marvis Frazier	November 25, 1983	10 wins
David Bey	March 15, 1985	14 wins
Carl Williams	May 20, 1985	16 wins

He was then deposed by Michael Spinks, on April 19, 1986. By coincidence Spinks was also undefeated, with 27 straight wins to his credit.

When former world champion George Foreman came to London to fight fellow American Terry Anderson, on September 25, 1990, his weight had ballooned to more than nineteen stones.

To be more comfortable he asked his hotel to install an extra sized bed to accommodate his giant frame.

The extra comfort must have had the desired effect because big George KO'd his opponent early in the first round.

Ben Caunt, bare-knuckle world champion around 1840, had a very distinguished landlord when he was a boy. His parents were tenants of Lord Byron.

Other undefeated heavyweight boxers who took part in world championship contests where, up to that time, their challenger was also undefeated are:

John L Sullivan	Muhammad Ali
James J Corbett	George Foreman
James J Jefferies	John Tate
Jack Munroe	Gerrie Coetzee
Joe Frazier	Mike Tyson
Buster Mathis	

There have been a few occasions when a double knockout has been recorded. There has even been an odd occasion when a boxer has been knocked out without the customary KO punch being landed. American bantamweight Harvey Gartley really wins the prize in this category.

In the early heats of a Golden Gloves tournament in Michigan, in February 1977, Gartley was making his boxing debut. His opponent was also engaging in his first public outing.

At the first bell Gartley came out bobbing, weaving, ducking and swinging wildly; so energetic was his action that with his first swing, he missed completely and fell over. He was so exhausted that he was unable to get to his feet – and the referee counted him out.

Forty seven seconds of the first round had elapsed and neither boxer had landed a single punch!

Eddie Vann clocked the fastest ever knockout when he stopped southpaw George Stern in 12 seconds – including the count. This record feat he achieved on the Randolph Turpin v Pete Mead bill at Harringay on November 15, 1949.

On the same bill Danny O'Sullivan did likewise to Belgian Michel Verhamme but Danny took his time about it – all of 56 seconds, including the count.

Harry Legge, Western Area lightweight champion in 1950, recalls one of the strangest bouts that he ever took part in, when he won by a knockout in the second round despite never throwing a single punch in that round.

The bout was in Penzance in May 1947 against Antonio Dobiji of Poland. Harry recalled that strange ending: 'I stopped him in round two – or rather he stopped himself.'

'The first round was a non-stop punch-up and I was prepared for a long tough battle. But at the start of the second round he threw himself across the ring and I went into a crouch to contain his attack. I lowered my head and crossed my gloves in front of me but he was coming so fast that he literally smashed his face into the top of my head.

I had not butted him; he had rammed his face into my skull so hard that his nose and eyebrows were cut and bleeding. He was stunned and although he was not counted out, it was ruled a knockout for me.

I did not throw a punch during that second round, yet I won by a KO.'

Billy Matthews, featherweight champion of Europe in 1922, was the brother of stage and screen actress, Jessie Matthews.

The four Buxton brothers of Watford, Alex, Laurie, Allan and Joe all appeared on the same bill at Bournemouth in 1949 and each of the brothers won their respective bouts.

Undefeated world heavyweight champion, Rocky Marciano was reported to have strange ideas about money. It is said that he used to keep vast amounts of cash around him and he would hide it in the most unusual places, sometimes forgetting where he had hidden it.

Years later after his death his daughter said in a magazine interview that she knew there was still a lot of money to be unearthed, if only it could be found – meanwhile, she said, she was almost penniless.

The only British title to be contested for on a Sunday was a flyweight championship. The bout took place on October 13, 1929 and was between Jackie Brown, who was to go on to world honours – and Bert Kirby.

Brown won by a third round KO.

Randolph Turpin carved a niche for himself in boxing history when he became middleweight champion of the world, on July 10, 1951.

But he was already a favourite with the British fans when he won the British middleweight crown on October 17, 1950. He later went on to win a Lonsdale Belt outright at light heavyweight.

Randy turned pro on the Bruce Woodcock – Gus Lesnevich bill, in London on September 17, 1946. He stopped his opponent in the first round and then went on to record eighteen more bouts before suffering his first reversal.

In a professional career 1946 to 1958, he clocked up 73 contests, losing only eight.

But he was already a record breaker before joining the paid ranks.

He was the first coloured boxer to become ABA champion. He was the first boxer to win a Junior and Senior title in the same year and, before he was eighteen years old he had won five ABA championships, three Junior and two Senior.

John Conte, undefeated light heavyweight world champion 1974 to 1977, remembers the time that he was really roughed up, back in his amateur days.

John, who was an amateur from eleven years old until he was twenty, was on a three match tour with an England squad in the USA. On this particular occasion he was in Columbus, Ohio and the weather was very hot indeed, something like 90 degrees in the shade. Then, as well as his opponent and the heat to contend with, it was discovered there was no water in his corner.

John says their chief coach, David Jones, didn't seem to notice the lack of water although the sponge was bone dry and rough as a bit of old leather.

'He just kept wiping my face with this dry sponge and my skin was getting more punishment from him than from my opponent, yet still he appeared not to notice. All the squad suffered the same treatment.

After that David was known as Brillo Pad Jones.

When Tommy Loughram fought Primo Carnera for the world heavyweight title in Miami on March 1, 1934, he was certainly the underdog.

Carnera outweighed Tommy by eighty pounds and stood nearly seven inches taller.

Never the less Tommy held his own for the full 15 rounds distance before losing the points decision.

An advertisement for Randolph Turpin in 1950, read thus:

'He's got a left hook second to none. In fact it's ten seconds to most!'

Randolph Turpin won the British, European and World middleweight titles all within the space of nine months.

Frank Bruno to Harry Carpenter: 'That's cricket, Harry. You get these kind of things in boxing.'

Bob Fitzsimmons, who started his working life as a blacksmith, made a small horseshoe for author Jack London's wife Charmain in 1910. Soon after he gave London a watch fob.

Fitzsimmons won the world title in 1897 and had retired from the ring in 1907 to go into showbusiness.

London reciprocated by writing Fitzsimmons a vaudeville sketch titled: Her Brother's Clothes.

Jokers

When Marvin Haglar came over to England to meet Alan Minter, with the world middleweight title at stake, the weigh-in took place earlier on the day of the bout, in the Wembley Arena.

There had been a lot of pre fight bad feeling between the two boxers which had spilled over to the crowd, that had turned up to witness the weigh-in.

Suddenly it was announced that Haglar was two pounds overweight.

The tension was relieved when, in order to make the weight, Haglar removed every stitch of clothing and stepped back onto the scales, this time completely naked.

'Cor,' cracked a joker from the crowd. 'Now we can see why you're two pounds overweight.'

Former world heavyweight champion, George Foreman is becoming as fast with the one-liners as he was with his hands. Since his spell at the top, decades ago, George has become as prolific as a gag cracker as he was as a ring warrior.

An example of his wit:

- 'When I'm fighting I don't see the other guys face, I see a great big juicy cheeseburger. That's what motivates me and helps me to knock them out quick.'
- 'My strategy is to try to hit them before they can duck.'
- More than thirty years after Muhammad Ali took his title in Zaire, Africa, jocular George was still telling people: ' He tricked me with his rope-a-dope trick .... you just lay on the ropes and let the dope tire himself out hitting you.'

Former welterweight champion Aaron Proir lost the sight of his left eye and with his sight went his licence to box.

But Wisconsin promoter Diana Lewis booked Prior on her show in Madison, on May 16, 1993, saying: ' If he is blind in one eye, he has still got another one.'

Proir won the bout by KO in the third round.

Marlon Starling is credited with those immortal words: ' I will fight anyone for free – as long as the money is right.'

~ 🜊 ~

Terry Downes, middleweight champion of the early 1960s, has a wicked sense of humour that he practices upon strangers to great effect. When he retired from the ring he became a successful businessman with a passion for expensive cars. He recalls two incidents involving this passion.

One day Terry was sitting in his parked car on the side of a very busy road, when a young policeman approached and asked him to get out.

'No chance, lad,' replied Downes.

'Come along sir, I want you out of the car please,' said the policeman again, this time very firmly.

'No hope,' said Downes.

'Well, why not?' asked the young policeman, at a loss for something else to say.

'Well son, if you're mug enough to stand out there with all that traffic whizzing past that's all right with me, but I'm not doing it.'

The remainder of the conversation was conducted in a nearby quiet side street.

~ 🜊 ~

Another time Terry was having a drink with friends in a Manchester pub when a policeman asked him to move his Rolls Royce.

'I can't really, not now,' he said, 'because I have been drinking and I don't want you to charge me with drink driving.'

The policeman made it clear that if the car was not moved it would be towed away, to which Downes replied: 'You can if you like mate, I've got another one.'

~ 🜊 ~

Asked on a television chat show, how he had lost all the money he'd earned from his days as a top class ring man, including a spell as world champ, wisecracking John Conte replied: ' I spent £175,000 on gambling; £200,000 on drugs; £300,000 on booze and £300,000 on chasing women – the rest I must have squandered.'

TERRY DOWNES

Former Middleweight Champion of the World, 1961
Former Middleweight Champion of Gt. Britain, 1958-59
and 1959-62
Winner outright of the Lord Lonsdale Belt

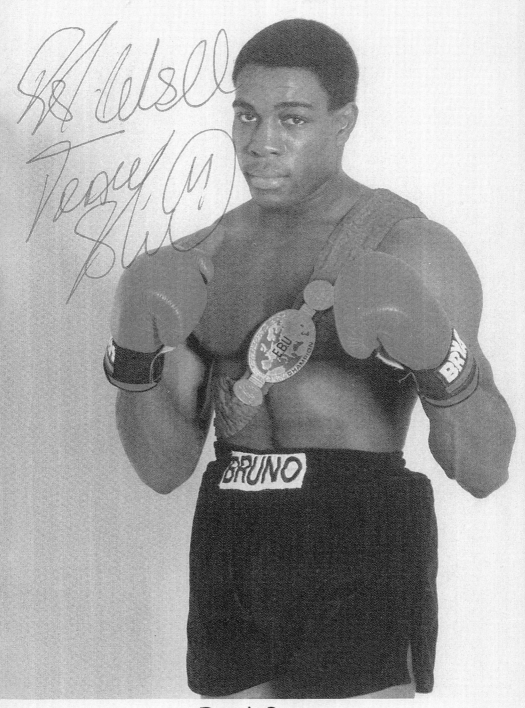

Frank Bruno

The first time Jackie Patterson met his opponent Theo Medina it was in Paris, on the afternoon of their scheduled contest in 1945. For a publicity stunt, the little Scot went into Medina's salon for a shave.

While Medina, the fighting barber was at work, Patterson laughingly remarked: 'You'd better be careful with that razor because if you cut me I'll knock you out tonight.'

Medina drew the back of the open razor across his customer's throat and came back with the witty reply: 'If I cut you Jackie, there will be no fight tonight.'

The Frenchman won on points.

~ ~

As referee Jack Hart inspected a bad cut on Bobby Bolands head between rounds, Scot Boland cracked: 'Don't worry ref, you'll not see any brains in there.'

~ ~

Gus Lesnevich, summing up the current light heavyweight division of which he was champion several years before, said: 'But for the fact that I can't make the weight and my wife won't let me, I might make a come back.'

~ ~

World middleweight champion of the early 1960s, Terry Downes has a mind that works as quickly as his hands used to during his heyday. He could always be relied upon to chip in with a wisecrack to suit any occasion.

When he was heading for America to meet Paul Pender for the world crown, he decided to travel by sea.

In a live interview on air, he was asked by a reporter why he chose to travel by sea rather than the much faster route of going by air. Quick as a flash Terry cracked: 'In case of accidents. I can swim much better than I can fly.'

~ ~

At a press conference, British based Hungarian heavyweight Joe Bugner was asked if he was prepared to fight certain named top flight boxers.

Flamboyant Joe replied: 'I would be prepared to fight Jesus Christ himself, if the money is right.'

From the body of the gathered pressmen came the witty return: 'Oh come on Joe. You're only saying that because you know he has got bad hands!'

~ 🜨 ~

A naïve young lady reporter, presumably at a loss of a question to ask now that she had his full attention, asked Terry Downes: 'When you are getting hurt in the ring, do you watch your opponents eyes or his hands?'

'His hands every time, luv,' he enlightened her. 'I ain't ever been hit by an eye in my life.'

~ 🜨 ~

Jock Malone, probably better remembered as a showman than a boxer, told boxing writers about his forthcoming bout with Frank Moody, in 1946.

He told them: 'If I lose to that Englishman, I'll jump into Boston Harbour.'

He did lose and, true to his word, he jumped off a bridge fifty feet into the water below.

Never one to miss a publicity chance, Jock had the stunt filmed by newsreel cameras and thousands came to watch him take his leap, which he did fully clothed.

~ 🜨 ~

Prior to when Archie Moore fought Willie Pastrano in 1962 'Ageless Archie', like everyone else, had to go through the standard pre-fight tests and weigh-in.

When it came to the eye test, Archie couldn't make out the letters on the chart and after the doctor brought this to his attention Archie joked: 'Well, Willie isn't going to be that far away!'

~ 🜨 ~

When Muhammad Ali, then still Cassius Clay, was called up for military service in the US army, he had trouble with the enlistment test, which he failed.

Having been told that he had failed, he cracked: 'I said I was the greatest, not the smartest!'

Possibly the greatest heavyweight fight to be staged at the old national Sporting Club, was between Peter Jackson and Paddy Slavin.

They were matched over twenty rounds for a £2,000 purse and Slavin wanted to fight for the lot. But Jackson stuck out for £250 to go to the loser. Jackson proved himself to be the better man and Slavin was knocked out in the tenth round.

When they met the next day for the customary handing over of the cheques, Jackson Said: ' You have got me to thank for having something to come, Paddy.'

A remark that made Slavin see red.

'I want no charity from no man,' he snarled, tearing his cheque into little pieces and throwing them at Jackson.

History records, however, that later in the day the Australian came back and humbly requested that another cheque be drawn up in his favour.

The last 45 round contest took place on April 5, 1915, in Havana, Cuba, between Jess Willard and Jack Johnson.

However, it didn't go the full distance because Willard cut it short by winning with a KO in the 26th round

When Dado Marino took the world flyweight title away from Englands Terry Allen, in Honolulu on August 1, 1950, the tiny Philipino at 33 years old was a grandfather.

In fact at that time he was the only grandfather to win a world title.

Of ten former world heavyweight champions that tried to regain their title from the man who had relieved them of it, only two were successful.

Floyd Patterson regained from Ingemar Johansson on March 13, 1961, in Miami then Muhammad Ali did the same from Leon Spinks, on September 15, 1978 in New Orleans.

The others that tried unsuccessfully were:

Fitzsimmons	from	Jefferies	July 25, 1902
Dempsey	from	Tunney	September 22, 1927
Charles	from	Walcott	June 5, 1952
Walcott	from	Marciano	May 15, 1953
Johansson	from	Patterson	March 13, 1961
Patterson	from	Liston	July 22, 1963
Liston	from	Ali	May 25, 1965
Weaver	from	Dokes	May 20, 1983
Holmes	from	M Spinks	April 19, 1986

The race for the fastest outright winning of the Lonsdale Belt goes ever onward. Howard Winstone (with his second Belt) and later Pat Cowdell made serious bids for the record but in more recent years the pace has really hotted up.

Welshman Robert Dickie must have thought he was in overdrive when he recorded his outright win in less than seven months. He put his notches on the coveted prize on April 19, 1986, July 30, 1986 and October 29, 1986.

But only a few short years later, former paratrooper Carl Crook grabbed the vacant lightweight title and recorded his first notch, on November 14, 1990. He then added the further two notches required on December 19, 1990 and April 24, 1991 – a total of only 161 days.

But hot on the heels of Crook came featherweight Colin McMillan, who later the same year made his assault on the record with his bouts toward a Lonsdale Belt for keeps taking place on May 22, 1991, September 4, 1991 and October 29, 1991 – twenty-four hours faster than Crooks recently established record.

It was Ted 'Kid' Lewis who first introduced gum shields into professional boxing. He had protruding front teeth and a dentist made him a special rubber pad to protect those teeth.

He wore his 'pad' whilst he was fighting in America and in one of his early bouts over there, his opponent Jack Britton raised a protest. Lewis was asked to remove the pad but refused.

When the American threatened to return to the dressing room, Lewis tore out his new gumshield and, throwing it into the centre of the ring, shouted at Britton; 'Come on then, I'll beat you without it.'

And he did.

The only double knockout recorded in England took place at Coventry on December 24, 1940. Local boxer Les Gascoigne was fighting Jim Boyce of Belfast in a preliminary bout. In the second round both boxers connected with right swings to the chin and both fell to the canvas, where they were counted out.

The referee added up the scorecard and found Boyce to be slightly ahead, so he awarded him the decision.

Johnny Prichett, British middleweight champion of the late 1960s, was so disappointed when he was disqualified unfairly, that he retired from the ring never to return.

Ray Robinson won the world middleweight championship of the world five times against:

1951 February 14	Jake LaMotta	13	RSF
1951 September 12	Randolph Turpin	10	RSF
1955 December 9	Carl Olson	2	KO
1957 May 1	Gene Fulmer	5	KO
1958 March 25	Carmen Basillio	15	PTS

He also defended against:

1952 March 13	Carl Olson	15	PTS
1952 April 16	Rocky Graziano	3	KO
1956 May 18	Carl Olson	4	KO

And lost his title in between to:

1951 July 10	Randolph Turpin	15	PTS
1957 January 2	Gene Fulmer	15	PTS
1957 September 23	Carmen Basilio	15	PTS
1960 January 22	Paul Pender	15	PTS

Then he had one more crack at regaining the title for a sixth time by taking Paul Pender a full 15 rounds distance, on June 10, 1960.

One of the most amazing things to happen in a ring must surely be the tragic ending of the bout that cost Luther McCarty his life.

The bout was in Calgary on May 24, 1913 and McCarty received the order to step back from a clinch in his bout with Arthur Pelkey. He did so and collapsed onto the canvas.

As the referee started the count, a shaft of sunlight broke through a hole in the roof and shone, like a spotlight, directly onto McCartys prone body. It was the first sunshine all day.

When the final ten was counted the shaft of sunlight vanished – and McCarty was dead.

The Real McCoy, a saying in common use today, was coined around 'Kid' McCoy, the world middleweight champion in 1897.

McCoy was an unpredictable boxer and fans would speculate whether they would see a dull uninspired bout or 'The Real McCoy'.

Benny Lynch, who ran through his fistic earnings almost as fast as he got them, once paid £100 and 1 shilling for a pound of grapes.

He was on his way to Liverpool for a return fight with Peter Kane and, as usual, he found difficulty in making the weight. Benny had not swallowed a drop of liquid for three days, so he must have been pretty thirsty.

While they were waiting for a train, Benny gave his trainer the slip and bought himself a pound of grapes for a shilling.

He managed to chew up most of them before his trainer could stop him and, as a result of eating those grapes, Benny was overweight at the weigh-in and paid a forfeit of £100. Which, pound for pound, must make those grapes the most expensive ever bought.

All boxers recognise the benefits to be gained from eating lots of steaks and red meat, with many a ring warrior having their meat bill sponsored by friendly butchers and meat wholesalers during their stint at the top.

But little Welshman Freddie Welsh proved that meat is not necessary for strength or stamina.

Freddie was the hard hitting British lightweight champion from 1909 to 1911 and again from 1912 to 1917 that his contempories feared. He also ruled the roost as world lightweight champion from 1914 to 1917 – and all this despite being a vegetarian.

For almost a century Freddie Welsh has been Britians only boxing vegetarian.

Al Singer won the world lightweight championship by a first round knockout and then lost the title just as spectacularly by being KOd himself in the first round of his first defence.

Both bouts took place in New York in 1930; the only two lightweight world championship bouts to be held that year.

Singer deposed champion Sammy Mandell in the first round on July 17 to take the title and was then deposed himself also in the first round, by Tony Canzoneri, on November 14.

This is the only case to date of a world champion winning and losing his title by a one round knockout each time – and in consecutive bouts.

The Ring

The Blackfriars Ring where most of the top names in British boxing had fought during the 1920s and 1930s was opened by Dick Burge in 1910 – and closed by Adolf Hitler in 1940.

The old place had been an ever present on the boxing scene for 30 years until German bombers scored a direct hit with their bombs in 1940. Then it was no more.

It could be said that Adolph Hitler really brought the house down.

Former lightweight champion, Dick Burge, promoter at The Ring, Blackfriars up until until his death during in World War One, was instrumental in getting boxing taken seriously by the national papers.

He persuaded the Daily Mirror to print a photograph of his top of the bill contestants and they obliged with the picture on the front page.

Soon after, on the crest of that small wave, special lights were installed above the ring to enable press photographers to get better pictures.

For the first half of the twentieth century The Ring had been Londons premier boxing venue. It was already an old building when boxing shows began and had started life many decades earlier as a chapel for religious services.

For the first few years that boxing was held there, the very bell that had summoned the congregation to their devotions was used to attract devotees of a different persuasion. It was used as the timekeeper's bell.

Bombardier Billy Wells was well and truly knocked out by his opponent Dick Smith in a bout at The Ring, London in 1915. Knocked right out of the ring in fact.

The referee, officiating from outside the ring, climbed in before starting the count, thereby giving Wells valuable extra seconds to recover. This he managed to do before the elongated count reached ten.

Wells took full advantage of his unexpected good fortune and knocked out Smith later in the bout.

When Mrs Bella Burge took over running boxing at The Ring, Blackfriars upon the death of her husband Dick – who died as the result of an air raid during World War One – she became the only woman boxing promoter in the world. Bella ran the place through good times and bad for twenty-two years and, in all those years never dodged paying her boxers, even at times having to sell her jewellery to make ends meet.

Bella Burge earned a reputation for fairness and honesty and she expected others to reciprocate those sentiments. One night, after a particular fearsome bout, the referee gave his decision and was booed out of the ring; the spectators were turning hostile.

Bella caught up with the referee and told him that he had made a big mistake. 'I know,' agreed the referee. 'I got the two contestants confused but I've given my verdict, I can't change it.'

'Oh yes you can,' said Bella. 'Get back up there and tell my patrons the truth. We all make mistakes, go back and tell them.' The referee did as advised and all was well.

Boxing historian Gilbert Odd recalled that Bella was a tough businesswoman but fair. In the prosperous days at The Ring, she held three shows a week, with sometimes extra shows on Monday or Saturday afternoon but with the coming of the depression of the 1930s, the old venue couldn't make ends meet.

She put all her money and most of her possessions into the business just to keep functioning. 'Make sure the boxers get their wages,' she insisted, 'after all, they take the punches, so they come first.'

She even took the step of closing down for renovations and as she put it: 'A good spring clean.' Then only a couple of days before the grand reopening the entire place was razed to the ground by a direct hit.

George Jones, who boxed as Jack O'Dare, was a great favourite at the Blackfriars Ring. An old poster inside the venue stated: 'Jack O'Dare. The greatest Fighting Machine ever seen at this hall. Just wind him up and he goes on forever.'

Jack Petersen, who was Boxing Board of Control president until his death in November 1990, started his professional career aged 21, on September 21, 1931.

He stopped his opponent in four rounds in a top of the bill clash.

Value for money Petersen boxed top of the bill in every professional bout he engaged in throughout his entire career.

Darlington welterweight Alan Hall was disappointed at the 1987 ABA Finals, where he boxed at lightweight.

He was sure that he had done enough to win so, as if to prove his point, he went back the following two years, 1988 and 1999 and won both times.

Lennox Lewis, the first British heavyweight world champion since Bob Fitzsimmons grabbed the title more than a century ago, started his career with the amateurs and contested two Olympic Games.

He had his first taste of Riddick Bowe, whom he stopped and Tyrell Biggs, who stopped him, in those Games.

Lennox sparred with an up and coming Mike Tyson as part of his preparation for the 1984 Los Angles Games.

Eventually he went on to win the coveted Gold Medal in the Seoul Olympics of 1988.

George Foreman celebrated his 25th birthday on January 22, 1973 by winning the world heavyweight championship. He stopped champion Joe Frazier in two rounds, at the National Stadium, Kingston, Jamaica.

Sugar Ray Leonard first threatened to retire after he won the Olympic Games Gold Medal in Montreal, in 1976. He was to repeat this threat four more times, in 1982, 1984, 1987 and finally in February 1991.

But the last time he really meant it and with something like a million dollars a year interest from the ring money he had invested, who could blame him.

Canadian Solly Cantor met fellow Canadian Don Mogard in digs, in New York early in his career. They went their separate ways and lost contact with each other until 40 years later when Solly was surprised to learn that they were living only a couple of miles apart, in South London.

Veteran campaigner Jerry Quarry, who first fought for the world title on April 27, 1968 when he made an unsuccessful attempt to unseat Cowboy Jimmy Ellis, applied to be relicensed as a boxer in California in 1990 – at the age of 45.

A contradiction in advice if ever there was.
An advertisement in Boxing dated (suspiciously) April 1, 1936 read thus:
GUM SHIELDS – must be made to model of your mouth. Ready made shields are useless, as every mouth is a different shape.
The genuine are only available from the inventor.
Mr J Marks, Gum Shield Co, 118 Notting Hill Gate, London
Price 10/6, crossed PO.
It is not necessary to call personally.
One wonders how they made the genuine models without a personal visit.

Father and son, Jim and Billy Kelly both held the British featherweight title.

Veteran trainer Eddie Futch, who was the guiding light behind the fortunes of Riddick Bowe, has guided eighteen boxers to world honours over the years.

Eddie was chief sparring partner to Joe Louis way back in 1934 but it was not until 1958 that he had his first world champion, in welterweight Don Jordon.

Young Johnny Owen, 'The Matchstick Man', became British champion at 21, he also became Commonwealth champion at 22 and at 23 he claimed a Lonsdale Belt outright. He repelled a challenge for his British and Commonwealth titles from John Seaney, who himself was until then unbeaten. He had also held the European title.

Gerry Cooney's hopes of becoming heavyweight world champion came to an end in the thirteenth round when his cornerman stepped into the ring. The bout, against Larry Holmes, was in Las Vegas on June 11, 1982 and at that time, was only the second time in boxing history that a world heavyweight title bout had ended in disqualification.

By coincidence the only other recorded occasion was 52 years earlier, almost to the day. That time it was June 12, 1930 in Yankee Stadium, New York, when Jack Sharkey fired a low blow into German Max Schemeling and was given his marching orders.

When former ABA champion Rod Douglas decided to turn pro in 1987, he did so in style. He dispatched his first four opponents all inside the distance and in four consecutive months – September, October, November and December.

When the Amateur Boxing Association came into being, Anthony Diamond soon stamped his authority on the lightweight division. He won the title three times in succession, in 1883, 1884 and 1885.

The following year, 1886, he was forced into competing in the heavyweight division... 'to give others a chance' – and just to show there were no hard feelings, he won the heavyweight title.

'FOREMAN VERSUS FIVE' was the billing in Toronto in 1975 when George Foreman fought five opponents on the same bill, in five three minute rounds.

Well remembered heavyweight world champion Floyd Patterson taught his son to box. Patterson junior learned his lessons well from one of the nicest and classiest boxers of all time. Tracy Patterson held the WBC featherweight title and, dad Floyd was the only former world champion to see his son win a world title.

Fancy being trained by a scarecrow? Over the years Jon Pertwee, of the television show Worzel Gummage fame, had done his bit toward helping up and coming boxers and at one stage even contemplated taking out a trainers license.

Hit Man, Thomas Hearns dispatched challenger Kemper Morton inside two rounds at Los Angeles on February 11, 1991 and picked up a winning purse of $50,000. He then donated the whole lot to the US servicemen that were fighting in the Middle East war.

The longest count of all time must surely be between two 'Kids' in 1902, when Kid Carter knocked out Kid McCoy.

For some reason McCoy was allowed to sleep on peacefully for more than sixty seconds. Then, to add insult to his opponent, he was saved by the bell,

Long time super featherweight champion Azumah Nelson finally succumbed in Las Vegas on May 8, 1994, when he lost his title to James Leija.

Ghanaian Nelson s ten year stint as WBC title custodian came to an end with a unanimous points decision at the end of twelve rounds.

The lightest heavyweight world champion (since modern records began) was Englishman Bob Fitzsimmons, who took the crown away from James J Corbett at Carson City on March 17, 1897. Bob, the Cornish blacksmith, weighed 12 stones 4 pounds.

The only other lightweight among heavies was Tommy Burns, who took the title from Marvin Hart on February 23, 1906. Tommy weighed 12 stones 11 pounds.

There are several boxers who have won the world heavyweight championship whilst in the 13 stones bracket, including Dempsey, Tunney and Schmeling.

Dave Finn fought at both National Sporting Clubs – Earls Court and Kings Street. Finn beat Dave Crowley five times but never got to fight for the Lonsdale Belt.

Sugar Ray Robinson, who incidentally disliked the tag Sugar, was a first class boxer as everyone knows. He was well liked by the fans, but not many boxers can claim to have been liked by their fellow boxers as well.

Tributes from some of the best remembered boxers of all time bear this out.

Brian London ignored the Control Board ruling forbidding him to fight for the heavyweight world title. He travelled to Indianapolis and challenged Floyd Patterson, on May 1, 1959.

Brian suffered a KO in the eleventh round.

Eric Boon beat Arthur Danahar in their much publicised lightweight title clash on February 23, 1939. Arthur had to wait seven years before he got his revenge, which he did on May 14, 1946, in five rounds, this time at welterweight.

Firsts

Pascual Perez was the first Argentinean to win a world title when he took the flyweight championship in Tokyo, on November 26, 1954.

By coincidence the champion he deposed, Yoshio Shirai, was the first Japanese to hold a world crown.

Perez went on to hold the title for more than five years. During that time he fought off nine challengers before succumbing himself on April 16, 1960, in Bangkok, to Pone Kingpetch.

Johnny Basham, British welterweight champion from 1914 to 1920 was the first welter to win a Lonsdale belt outright.

Floyd Patterson was the first Olympic Gold Medallist to go on to win the heavyweight world championship.

He was the youngest boxer (until he conceded that record to Mike Tyson) to win the heavyweight crown and he was the first heavyweight boxer to regain the world title.

Quite a record.

But a record that he is not so proud of is that of being decked 17 times as champion. However modest, likable Floyd argues: ' I was never counted out on the canvas – so, if I hold the record for going down then I must hold the record for getting up!'

A very good point.

Vic Toweel was the first South African boxer to win a world title. Toweel had a rapid rise to fame, taking just over a year as a professional to gain the world bantamweight crown. However, his success was not easily gained – he had to take the title away from long time holder Manuel Ortiz, a feat that many other challengers had failed to do.

The first heavyweight bout of the twentieth century featured two James Js.

It was staged at Coney Island, New York on May 11, 1900 and champion James J Jefferies repelled the challenge of former champion James J Corbett, by a twenty- third round knockout.

The aptly named Harry Legge boxed with a withered leg, courtesy of a bout of polio when he was five years old. Harry boxed in the booths and on the professional circuit for many years. He took part in more than 160 official bouts and with his booth workload, perhaps many hundreds more.

Billy Bolton boxed professionally in the early 1930s despite the handicap of an artificial leg.

Wilfred Benitez became the youngest boxer ever to hold a world title when he took the world junior welterweight championship on March 6, 1976, in San Juan, Porto Rico. He was 17 years and 7 months old.

The British championship belts were introduced in 1909 by Lord Lonsdale and were known as National Sporting Club Challenge Belts. In 1936 control passed to the British Boxing Board of Control and the Belts were renamed Lonsdale Belts.

The small men won the race to outright ownership of a Belt, with featherweight Jim Driscoll being the first boxer to own a NSC Belt and lightweight Eric Boon doing likewise with the first BBBofC Belt.

But later they were both overshadowed by a big man – heavyweight Henry Cooper holds a record three Lonsdale Belts won outright, which is the most any boxer has ever won

To win a Belt outright a boxer must score three victories in championship matches at the same weight. These wins need not be consecutively. A boxer can lose his title and regain it with each win counting toward his three wins.

These days only one Belt is awarded immaterial of how many wins a boxer achieves – after his three obligatory wins, of course.

When welterweight Lloyd Honeyghan regained his crown from Jorge Vaca in the Wembley Arena in March 1988, he was the first British boxer to do so since Ted 'Kid' Lewis 70 years previously.

When Manuel Ortiz won the world bantamweight title, in Hollywood on August 7, 1942, he became the first Mexican ever to win a world title – and this despite actually having been born in California.

Never-the-less he proved to be a splendid boxing ambassador for Mexico and, apart from a small hiccup between January 6 and March 11, 1947, he held the title from then until May 31, 1950. In his first spell as world champ he held the title for four and a half years, repelling 15 challengers in that period.

February 10, exactly two years after losing his world title to Buster Douglas in Tokyo, Mike Tyson was in court in Indiana to hear that his career had been further defeated by 18 year old Desiree Washington – the girl he was accused of raping.

World flyweight champion of 1966, Walter McGowan was the first Scots boxer to beAwarded an MBE in the Queens Birthday Honours List.

~ 𝄞 ~

Johnny King, Walter McGowan and Charlie Magri were all awarded a Lonsdale Belt outright without having to take the customary three wins. It was found that there was no one in their class at the respective times for them to make the stipulated defences against.

King fought twice for his Belt before challengers ran out, with McGowan and Magri fighting only once apiece for theirs.

~ 𝄞 ~

The first black man to win a British crown was Dick Turpin. Dick took the middleweight title from Vince Hawkins, on June 28, 1948.

The fight over 15 rounds at Birmingham was the first time coloured boxers were allowed to contest the British titles. Prior to that they had only been permitted to contest Empire titles.

When Horace Notice put the third notch on his Lonsdale Belt, making it his for keeps, he was the first heavyweight to do so since Henry Cooper more than twenty years earlier.

~ ᛉ ~

Hogan 'Kid' Bassey who won the featherweight world championship on June 24 1957 in Paris, was awarded the MBE. He was the first Nigerian boxer to receive the decoration.

~ ᛉ ~

When Jack Johnson defended his world heavyweight crown against Jim Johnson, on December 19 1913 in Paris, not only did both contestants have the same name but it was also the first time two black men had fought each other for the world heavyweight championship. Champion Jack Johnson was forced to retire hurt at the end of the tenth round but, for some reason the bout was declared a draw, thereby allowing him to hold on to his crown.

~ ᛉ ~

Payao Poontarat, Bronze Medal winner in the Montreal Olympics of 1976 and Thailands first Olympic medal winner, used to sell flowers to passers by on the roadside.

He started his career with Thai boxing in his native Bangkok in 1975 and by 1983 had progressed to western style boxing and the flyweight world title.

~ ᛉ ~

Nel Tarlton and Johnny King are the only two boxers to have won both a Lonsdale Belt and a NSC Belt outright.

~ ᛉ ~

Prince Naseem Hamed criticised flamboyant Chris Eubank for copying his act of entering the ring by vaulting over the top rope.

But while these two new boys continue to argue, they might reflect on the fact that Terry Downes was doing that same thing more than thirty years earlier.

Talk about dedication: Little Eric Boon rode his bicycle from his home town of Chatteris all the way to the Devonshire Sports Club, in Hackney, London for his professional debut.

That certainly was dedication and it was almost certainly a first.

~ 🏃 ~

To date there has only been one pair of brothers to win a Lonsdale Belt each, outright. The brothers to achieve this remarkable feat are the Finnegan boys, Chris and Kevin.

Chris claimed his three scalps, as a light heavyweight, on January 24, 1971; March 3, 1973 and October 14, 1975.

Middleweight Kevin climbed his three steps to the record books and a Lonsdale Belt for keeps on February 11, 1974; May 31, 1977 and November 6, 1979

~ 🏃 ~

Englishman Owen Moran holds the distinction of being the first man to knockout the famous Battling Nelson.

~ 🏃 ~

Razor Ruddock, Canadian domiciled Jamaican heavyweight had a claim to fame that is hard to beat.

In Jamaica he was reputed to be able to knock mango fruit out of the tree by throwing stones at them. This feat he was said to be able to do consistently with his first shot.

~ 🏃 ~

Heavyweight world champion Gene Tunney has the distinction of having a cocktail named after him. Simply called The Gene Tunney Cocktail, it consists of the following:

One dash orange juice

One dash lemon juice

$1/3$ dry vermouth

$2/3$ gin

Shake well and strain into a cocktail glass.

One wonders if it packs a wallop like the famous man himself.

Joe Louis, on Ray Robinson:

'He was the best fighter that ever lived, pound for pound. He sure could punch. Even when he was backing away he was still dangerous with his left hook.'

Muhammad Ali, on Ray Robinson:

'I'm the best ever heavyweight champion but I would have to say Ray Robinson was the best boxer ever.'

Floyd Patterson, on Ray Robinson:

'Clay (Ali) had great legs but couldn't punch. Marciano could punch, but there was only one fighter that could do it all. That was Ray Robinson. He was the greatest fighter ever.'

Tributes indeed. But Robinson could account for himself.

He won the Golden Gloves featherweight title in 1939 and the lightweight title in 1940.

Then he turned professional and went on to win the world middleweight title an incredible five times.

Heavyweight champions undefeated when they won the world title:

Rocky Marciano	42 wins	*Also:*	
George Foreman	37 wins	Tony Tucker	33 wins, 1 draw
John L Sullivan	34 wins	Micheal Dokes	25 wins, 1 draw
Larry Holmes	27 wins	Pinklon Thomas	24 wins, 1 draw
Micheal Spinks	27 wins	James J Jefferies	11 wins, 2 draws
Mike Tyson	27 wins	James J Corbett	9 wins, 4 draws
Ingemar Johansson	21 wins	Leon Spinks	6 wins, 1 draw.
Tony Tubbs	20 wins		
Muhammad Ali	19 wins		
Joe Frazier	19 wins		
John Tate	19 wins		

Boxings 'Mr Nice Guy' Floyd Patterson has been known to show concern for a stricken opponent, as he demonstrated in New York on June 20, 1960, when he regained the world crown from Ingemar Johansson, via a fifth round stoppage.

As soon as Johansson had been counted out, Floyd was the first to rush to his aid.

But far earlier in his professional career Floyd laid the foundation for his 'Gentleman' tag when, having knocked out an opponents gum shield, he watched the confused boxer scrambling around more intent upon retrieving his lost gum shield than continuing the bout.

Seeing that he couldn't do it, Floyd picked up the gum shield and handed it back.

Mouthpiece back in place the bout continues.

At Madison Square Garden in March 1948, French glamour boy Marcel Cerdan floored his opponent Laverne Roach, but crafty Roach pulled Cerdan down with him, as he fell.

By the time the referee and timekeeper had agreed that Roach was knocked down and had not slipped, an incredible twenty-four seconds had elapsed.

Jack Broughton, the man that has gone down in history as 'The Father of the English School of Boxing', did a lot to clean up the sports image during his ten year reign 1740-50. He is also credited with inventing boxing gloves, or mufflers as they were then called.

Broughton, the third boxing champion after James Figg and George Taylor, drew up boxings first set of recognised rules and these were officially adopted on August 16, 1743.

His rules were to govern boxing for the next 140 years or so, until the Marquis of Queensbury Rules took over around the time of the formation of the National Sporting Club, in 1891.

The Queensbury rules are reported to have been devised in 1865 and revised in 1890. They have remained the mainstay of British boxing ever since.

But unlike Broughton, it is said that the Marquis of Queensbury did not actually write the rules that have carried his name. Reports from the period state that they were drawn up by a fellow student of Queensbury's acquaintance.

Paddy Ryan had a dream debut for his first ever professional bout. He won the heavyweight championship of the world.

On May 30, 1880 he beat Joe Goss over 86 rounds, in West Virginia.

Unfortunately his glory was short lived because in his very next bout he lost the title.

After revelling in his newfound fame and glory for around nine months, He came unstuck at the hands of John L Sullivan in a short nine rounds, on February 7, 1882, in Mississippi City.

Making Ryan the only man to have won the world title in his first professional bout - and lose it in his next.

After the much publicised fight between Thomas Hearns and Sugar Ray Leonard that ended in a draw, Leonard stated he should have got the decision. He was so annoyed at not getting the verdict that he sacked five of his company.

The 'fiasco fight' was reported to have brought in about 65 million dollars, which was also not good news because that figure was well below the estimated total.

Al Wodgast's moment of glory came when he took the world lightweight title in an action filled 40 round bout against Battling Nelson, in February 1910.

But his reminisces were to be short lived unfortunately for him because his memory failed him a couple of years later and he was hospitalised in a Californian sanatorium in 1927.

From then until his death in 1955 at the age of 67, he continually hallucinated that he was soon to meet Joe Gans for the world championship – although Gans had died many years previously.

The Empress Hall, Earls Court programme for the 1951 season showed two boxing gloves on the cover – both for the left hand.

Bobby Boland took a ten round points decision over British bantamweight champion Danny O'Sullivan, at the Empress Hall on October 10, 1950 and that signalled a change of luck for him.

For prior to that bout he had his head split open by a sparring partner; bruised his hand on the heavy bag in the gym; skinned his hand in a fall whilst out on roadwork, and then topped it all by slipping over and sustaining a sprained ankle.

Roberto Duran, the durable destroyer in many epic battles, drew to the close of his fistic career owing one and a half million dollars to the tax man.

Manuel Ortiz started his boxing career by standing in as a last minute substitute in an amateur show in 1936. He liked the experience so much that he entered the Golden Gloves competition the following year and won the flyweight title. The year after that he turned professional and soon went on to world honours.

British featherweight champion, Floyd Havard received some medical advice for his hand injury from a very strange quarter.

A local farmer suggested that he soak his hand in a stream on the farm.

'It always work when my horses have an injury,' he said.

When Tony Wilson met Steve McCarthy at Southampton in 1989 with the British light heavyweight championship being the prize, things were not all going his way.

Suddenly he received help from an unexpected quarter when his mother jumped into the ring and began belting his opponent over the head with her shoe.

John Tate, who won the WBA world heavyweight championship in October 1979 is reportedly unable to read or write. It would have been more understandable in the Eighteen Hundreds but surely not these days.

A few days before their famous 1939 championship fight, Arthur Danahar met Eric Boon in a milk bar and, over a cup of coffee, he said: 'Here's to our forthcoming bout, Eric. May the best man win.'

To which Boon responded: 'I will!'

History records that he did, with the fight being stopped in the 14th round of a thrilling contest.

Willie Pep lost his world featherweight crown to Sandy Sadler on October 29, 1948, by a knockout in the fourth round and that was the first time he had taken the count in 137 contests, reaching back more than eight years.

Stuart Fleet KO'd Robert Norton in Walsall on September 30, 1993.

It was a cruiserweight contest but there was no time to cruise on that night. Both men visited the canvas and the whole bout was over in twenty five seconds.

Young, Younger, Youngest

Liverpudlian Peter Fallon beat champion Bert Hornby for the North Central lightweight title over twelve rounds, at Liverpool on April 18, 1948 – then had to do it all over again the following year because it was found that he was too young to compete for a title.

~ 🦋 ~

Peter duly obliged and the second set-to on August 25, 1949 proved to be a copy of the original bout, with him taking the title yet again – and again over the twelve rounds route

~ 🦋 ~

Georges Carpentier won his first championship, as an amateur flyweight, when he was twelve years old and he had his first professional bout when he was thirteen.

~ 🦋 ~

Teddy Baldock, world bantamweight champion in the mid 1920s, started boxing for pay a couple of months before his 14th birthday.

~ 🦋 ~

Iron Mike Tyson became the youngest boxer to win the heavyweight world championship when he knocked out Trevor Berbick in Las Vegas on November 11, 1986.

After taking the WBC title from Berbick in two rounds, it took him the full twelve rounds distance to get the WBA version of the title, via Bonecrusher Smith, in Las Vegas on March 7, 1987.

Still in Las Vegas, he acquired the IBF title courtesy of Tony Tucker, on August 1, 1987, again over the twelve rounds distance.

This gave him all three titles and was the first time the heavyweight championship had been unified since 1978.

Iron Mike was then 23 years old. He had taken part in 37 bouts and had clocked up 37 wins – 33 of them via the KO route.

~ 🦋 ~

The youngest champion was Wilfred Benitez, American light welterweight at 17 years and 173 days.

Jack O'Dare
Aged 16

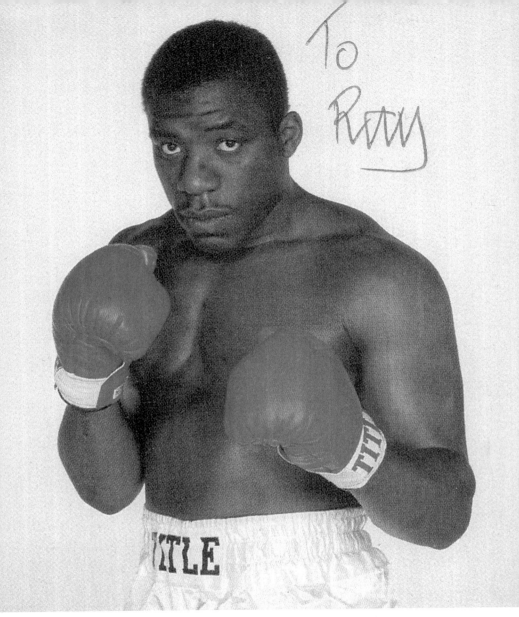

To Rory

GARY MASON

good luck GJ Mason

In February 1993 when Ray Mercer fought Jesse Ferguson at Madison Square Garden it was alleged that the ring microphone picked up Mercers voice offering Ferguson a bribe.

Later it was announced by the New York District Attorney's office that Mercer would be charged and, if found guilty, would receive a sentence heavier than the six years handed out to Mike Tyson for rape.

This prompted outspoken boxing publisher Bert Randolph Sugar to comment: 'It's curious that Ferguson was not indicted for failure to report a bribe.'

He was referring back to the time when Rocky Graziano was suspended in New York for not reporting a bribe.

Sugar cracked: 'Hell, any lawyer – except Vincent Fuller, who ineptly defended Tyson – could get Mercer off.'

To top it all, when a reporter asked whether this affair was connected to organised crime, a boxing wit shouted: 'No, this was disorganised crime.'

Lennox Lewis had his first taste of world honours way back in 1983 when, as an eighteen year old, he won the world junior championship, in the Dominican Republic.

Londoner Jesse Keough trained hard and long for his first pro fight and then spent less than half a minute in front of the fans who had come to witness his debut at London's York Hall, on April 27, 1994.

Keough went on the attack from the bell and bludgeoned his opponent, Warren Stephens into submission in just twenty seconds.

What a dream, if somewhat short lived, debut.

Promising Welsh boxer Miguel Matthews career was brought to an abrupt end by an out-of-ring accident. The Swansea boy trapped his arm in a machine at the mine where he worked.

The longest bare knuckle fight in Australia took place in Melbourne, in November 1855, between James Kelly and Jonathon Smith. The bout lasted six hours and fifteen minutes.

Old timer Jem Mace, unofficially styled Father of English Boxing, was a very popular man in Australia. When he was leaving after a tour of that country, his Australian admirers presented him with a gold brick.

The brick was inscribed: This is a brick and you are another.

Cockney boxer Pat O'Keefe added the final touch to his National Sporting Club Belt by beating Bandsman Blake in London, whilst the worst air raid of the World War One was going on outside.

The world famous Madison Square Gardens hosted boxing for the last time on July 8, 1993, in front of just 1,700 fans. Ironically the last man to be knocked out on a Garden promotion was Marcel Huffaker – whose nickname was Bedtime.

The night before the Robinson v Doyle fight for the world welterweight crown, in June 1947, Ray Robinson dreamed that he knocked out Jimmy Doyle and that Doyle died as a result of that KO.

The following morning Robinson asked to cancel the bout but after long negotiations the boxing commissioners and a priest persuaded him to carry on with the bout.

The scheduled fight went ahead at the allocated time and, just as in the dream, Robinson caught Doyle with a left hook and Doyle dropped dead at his feet.

When Terry Norris beat the legendary Sugar Ray Leonard in Madison Square Gardens on February 9, 1991, he took no satisfaction from the fact.

Despite an absolutely one sided affair where Norris scored at least four 10-8 rounds, he was sad to have beaten the veteran champion of five different weights – and eleven years his senior.

Norris said after the bout: 'It was sad victory because he was my idol.' Then he added: 'He's still my idol.'

Freddie Mills handed Len Harvey his one and only knockout. This was when they met at Tottenham, London on June 20, 1942.

In the second round Mills achieved the feat that others had failed to do and earned himself the British and Empire heavyweight titles in the process.

There is no such thing as a Knockout in British boxing.

The British Board of Control rules state: 'A contestant failing to continue the contest at the expiration of ten seconds shall not be awarded any marks for that round and the contest shall then terminate.'

For the third defence of his WBO world middleweight title against Steve Collins on May 11, 1994, champ Chris Pyatt told the press: 'This one will not go the distance.'

He proved to be something of a prophet on that night in the Sheffield International Arena because the bout did not go the distance.

Unfortunately it was Pyatt who was ruled out.

When Marvin Haglar, former middleweight world champion, was inducted into the International Hall of fame, in June 1993, he said: 'Being inducted is the final chapter in my career in boxing.'

Most would argue that his long stint as undisputed world champ from 1980 to 1987 bears testament to a first class achievement.

Rough and tough sailor, Tom Sharkey took up boxing and almost straight away became a force to be reckoned with among the heavyweights of his day.

One night when he was in the money a friend persuaded him to go to a high class restaurant and have a dozen oysters.

He enjoyed then so much that the next night he went back and ordered the same again.

'I'm sorry,' said the waiter, 'we're out of oysters what about a lobster?'

'OK, bring me a dozen,' demanded the old sailor.

'We usually find one is enough for a customer,' said the waiter a bit warily but at the same time trying to be helpful. So Sharkey asked for the biggest one they had.

When the lobster was set before him, Sharkey looked at it suspiciously. He lifted it off the plate, inspected it thoroughly and then growled: 'It's a bit light to starboard, ain't it?'

'Well it has lost a feeler,' agreed the waiter, 'but these fellows are always fighting and that often happens.'

'Take it away,' roared the fighting sailor. 'I ain't interested in losers, bring me the winner.'

During his reign as world middleweight champion, flamboyant Chris Eubank didn't much care for the black tarmac outside his home, so he paid for enough paving slabs to cover the hundred yard stretch of pavement that boarded his property, and Brighton council obliged by laying them for him instead.

Bruiser was one of the last of the 'old-time' fighters, he never seemed to be entirely up to date as he shuffled around the gym and promoters office, picking up a few bob by sparring and sweeping up at the end of the day. He was never likely to be champion or even a contender even though he had served a long apprenticeship and had the usual trophies to show for it – cauliflower ears and a bent nose etc.

He was quite happy in his own small way except for one thing, his wife. His lack of money to bring home gave her cause for complaint and she exercised that right continually. Nag, nag, nag all the time and always about money.

Until one week when Bruiser had a couple of last minute substitute jobs and was in the money.

'I've got a bit of spare cash now, my love,' he told her. 'So what would you like me to buy for your birthday?' Suddenly she was a changed person.

'That is very kind of you Bruiser my dear,' she replied. 'What I would really like is a coffin. A good quality job with brass handles and a plaque with my name on it, then I shall be happy in the knowledge that when my time comes, I can go out in style.'

True to his word Bruiser bought his wife the coffin that she desired and it had pride of place in their spare room, where she dusted and polished it every day. Things appeared to be much improved between them and soon a year had gone by.

'What will you buy me for my birthday this year my love?' she asked sweetly.

'Aw, leave orf gal,' said the old timer indignantly. 'You ain't used last years present yet!'

Dan Donnelly had just become champion of England and the Duke of Clarence, a royal patron of the prize ring, sent for him.

Afraid that the uneducated Irishman might commit some breach of etiquette his sponsor instructed him beforehand.

'When you address the Duke, you always begin by saying Your Grace,' he was told.

When Donnelly returned home his sponsor accused him of begging off the Duke.

'Didn't I tell you not to cadge off him and remember to say Your Grace.'

Donnelly protested that he didn't forget. 'We shook hands and I said: for what we are about to receive..... and before I could finish, he gave me a guinea.'

Members of Parliament

Colin Moynihan, Minister for Sport in the late 1980s – early 1990s, was a first class amateur boxer whilst at University.

As a bantamweight he boxed for Oxford against Cambridge in the Varsity Matches of 1975 and 1976.

The following year he changed sport to cox the Oxford crew to victory in the annual Oxford–Cambridge Boat Race of 1977. Colin's crew won by seven lengths in a time of 19 minutes 53 seconds.

But it was not all fun and games because, having boxed at eight stones seven pounds, he had to lose a stone for the Boat Race.

This he achieved by shovelling hops in a nearby Mortlake brewery.

~ ~

Andrew Bowden MBE, former Member of Parliament for Brighton Kemptown, Sussex, was a handy schoolboy battler in his youth and later, in the army he went on to box for his regiment, The Royal Corps of Signals. However, all this athletic activity did not impress his public school headmaster, The Right Reverend George Snow, of Ardingly College.

On one occasion the Reverend Snow, who was over six feet six inches tall, bumped into Bowden in the school corridor and told him: 'You are a leader in this school Bowden, you lead the troublemakers.'

Undoubtedly Reverend Snow would be amazed to learn that these days Andrew Bowden is a member of the School Governing Body in addition to having been a Member of Parliament.

Indeed, when the reverend gentleman learned that Andrew Bowden had been elected as an MP a few years ago, he said: 'The thought of being governed by Bowden fills me with gloom.'

~ ⚔ ~

Bare knuckle fighter of the early 1880s John Gully started his career in fisticuffs after being released from debtors' prison. He went on to become champion before going on to be a successful racehorse owner and having two Derby winners to his credit.

Later still, he became speaker of the House of Commons.

When Dick Turpin joined the professional ranks, in the late 1930s, his two younger brothers Jackie and Randolph would sometimes feature on the same programme.

Billed as Alexander and Moses, the two youngsters who were still of school age, would box exhibition bouts.

Such crowd pleasers were the pair of schoolboys that often nobbins after their bout would amount to more than big brother Dick's legitimate purse.

Silver Belt holder Bert 'Kid' Freeman also recalled the old dodge of having someone in the audience throw a couple halfpennies in the ring after his bouts. That started the ball rolling and those nobbins made him sometimes as much as his purse to add to his take-home pay.

Jack Edwards, nationally known as 'Chatham Jack', had a first class career as a well respected trainer that spanned almost thirty years until his death on Good Friday 1955.

As well as running two training schools Jack was also chief whip and second at Rochester Casino and such was his fame that visiting boxers would ask for Jack to be in their corner.

As well as his six sons, Jack trained several top class boxers including Eddie Vann, the heavyweight who is credited with the fastest knockout of all time. This came about when Vann laid low George Stern in twelve seconds – including the count, on the Mead v Turpin bill at Harringay on November 15, 1949.

'Chatham Jack' had two young sons, Alfie and George, that he introduced to the public at a very tender age. Known as Chatham Jack's Midgets he travelled all over the country with them giving displays of four one-minute rounds. Primo Carnera once carried one of the midgets into the ring on his shoulder.

Muhammad Ali has been dubbed 'The Greatest' mostly through his own self -promotion and he will undoubtedly always be known by that name. But there was a man who could truthfully lay claim to the name.

A middleweight who fought in America in the late 1950s, until his death in the mid 1960s, was actually named Greatest Crawford.

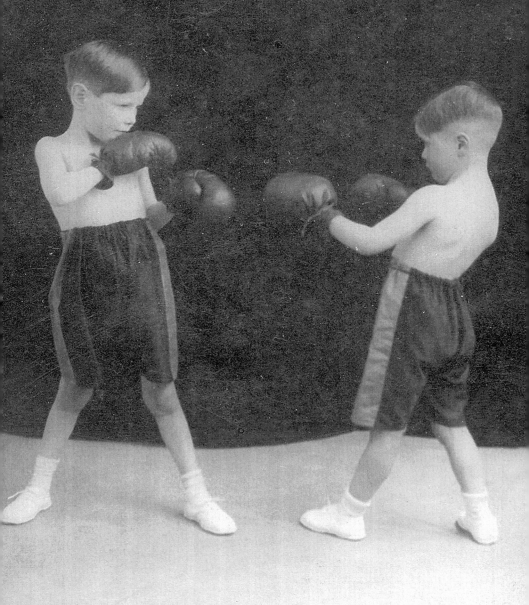

Chatham Jack's Midgets

AGREEMENT.

I, W. A. Pullum, of 5, Church Street, Camberwell Green, S.E., agree to undertake the management of the professional boxing affairs of WILLIAM ROBERT STORRIE (boxing as "SEAMAN BILL STORRIE"), and to make myself responsible for all that that means for a period of twelve months from the date of APRIL 22nd, 1934. At the end of which time the said WILLIAM ROBERT STORRIE to be allowed the option of continuing for a further period to be mutually agreed - or discontinuing without any further liability or obligation to himself.

The total commission to be deducted from Seaman Bill Storrie's earnings as a boxer during this period not to exceed 20%.

W. A. Pullum.

I, WILLIAM ROBERT STORRIE, agree that the above meets with my full approval, and I hereby empower W. A. PULLUM so to act on my behalf.

William R. Storrie.

WITNESSED BY   *William John Storrie*
22/4/1934   *William Stanley Pullum.*

120

When Joe Bowker took the bantamweight world title from Frankie Neil, on October 17, 1904, in London. He became world champion before he was British champion.

Fred Pursey took the unusual route to the Kent featherweight championship – he just claimed it. Fred placed an ad in his local newspaper, the Kent Messenger, claiming the title, inviting anyone disputing his claim to challenge him. One challenger came forward but withdrew from the proposed decider at the Devonshire Club and Pursey was accepted as title holder.

There were, by coincidence, five heavyweight world champions with the same forename – James J.

They were of course:
James J Corbett
James J Jeffries
James J Willard
James J Braddock
and Gene Tunney. Yes, Genes real name was James Joseph Tunney!

Jocko Pett, southpaw amateur of the 1940s through to the 1970s, has a claim that is unlikely ever to be bettered. The Kent based lightweight battler boxed his way through 621 bouts before calling it a day.

For army service he served as a PTI, which meant he was a fit man. On one occasion, having missed the team coach, Jocko rode his bicycle to the show – a distance of something like twenty-five miles – before taking part in his scheduled bout.

Being amateur, prizes were usually tea and coffee sets and the almost obligatory canteens of cutlery. Jocko normally won the lion's share, which he would try to sell before leaving the venue.

There have been a few occasions where a boxer has taken on five opponents in the same night. Bob Fitzsimmons started the ball rolling when he knocked out all five of his opponents. Later Sam Baxter equalled the feat.

John C Heenan's championship belt from the classic Heenan v Sayers battle of April 17, 1860 and old time British champion Charlie Mitchells belt, along with the Lonsdale Belt that rightly belonged to Jack Petersen but eluded him from May 23, 1932, for the rest of his life, were on display at the Museum of Mankind, London, before being returned to the Control Board.

World Bareknuckle Champions

1719   James Figg
1730   Tom Pipes
1734   George Taylor
1740   Jack Broughton *(Buried in Westminster Abbey)*
1750   Jack Slack *(Grandson of James Figg)*
1760   Bill Stevens
1761   George Meggs
1762   Baker Milsom
1765   Tom Jachau
1764   Bill Darts
1764   'Waterman' Lyons *(Retired after 2 weeks)*
1769   Bill Darts
1771   Peter Corcoran *(First Irish champion - he beat Darts in less than one minute - shortest ever heavy-weight title fight)*
1776   Harry Sellers
1780   Duggan Fearns
1783   Tom Johnson *(Christened Thomas Jockling)*
1791   Benjamin Brain *('Big Ben')*
1794   Daniel Mendoza *(First Jewish champion)*
1795   'Gentleman' Jackson
1795   William Hooper
1803   Jem Belcher *(Grandson of Jack Slack)*
1805   Henry Pearce
1807   John Gully *(Elected champion)*
1808   Tom Cribb *(Dec 18 - first title fight between black and white men (v Tom Molineaux))*
1822   Tom Spring *(Elected champion. Real name Thomas Winters)*
1824   Tom Cannon
1825   Jem Ward *(First boxer to receive a championship belt)*
1827   Peter Crawley *(Retired - held title only 2 days)*
1828   Jem Ward *(Reclaimed title)*
1833   James 'Deaf' Burke *(First English champion to fight in America)*
1839   William Thompson *('Bendigo')*
1840   Ben Caunt
1841   Nick Ward
1845   William Thompson *('Bendigo')*
1849   Tass Parker
1850   William Perry *('The Tipton Slasher')*
1851   Harry Broome
1853   Nat Langham
1856   Tom Paddock
1858   Tom Sayers
1858   Sam Hurst
1860   John Heenan *(First American heavyweight champ to be matched against British champ)*
1861   Jem Mace
1863   Tom King *(Retired)*
1863   Jem Mace
1868   Mike McCoole
1870   Tom Allen
1871   Jem Mace *(Retired)*
1873   Tom Allen *(Retired)*
1876   Joe Goss
1880   Paddy Ryan *(Won championship in his first professional bout and lost it in his next)*
1882   John L. Sullivan